AGRARIAN REFORM AND
SOCIAL TRANSFORMATION

About the Author

Professor Rehman Sobhan is one of South Asia's most distinguished economists. He was born in Calcutta in 1935 and educated at Cambridge University (1953–56). After teaching at Dhaka University for 17 years, he became Research Director of the Bangladesh Institute of Development Studies in 1974, and subsequently Director General, until his retirement in 1989. He was also elected President of the Bangladesh Economic Association (1983–85).

He was closely involved with his country's struggle for independence and, upon its conclusion, was appointed a member of the government's Planning Commission on which he served for two and a half years. More recently, following the fall of General Ershad, he became a member of the interim government which presided over the country's elections and held the Planning and External Relations portfolio.

He has also served in a number of prestigious international positions. He has been a member of the UN Committee for Development Planning, the Governing Council of the United Nations University and the board of the United Nations Research Institute for Social Development.

Apart from a large number of scholarly articles and papers published over 30 years of professional activity, Professor Sobhan is the author of eight books. He has concentrated, in particular, on the role of public enterprise in Asian economies, questions of aid dependence versus self-reliance and South–South cooperation, as well as poverty and agrarian reform. In addition to a series of volumes which he has recently edited on the current state of the Bangladeshi economy, his books include:

Basic Democracies, Works Programme, and Rural Development in East Pakistan (Oxford University Press, Pakistan, 1968)

The Crisis of External Dependence: The Political Economy of Foreign Aid to Bangladesh (University Press, Dhaka, 1982, and Zed Books, London, 1984)

Public Enterprise and the Nature of the State: The Case of South Asia (Centre for Social Studies, Dhaka, 1983)

Poverty and Agrarian Reform in the Philippines (FAO, Rome, 1984)

Trade, Planning and Rural Development: Essays in Honour of Rural Islam (co-edited with A. R. Khan) (Macmillan, London, 1990)

REHMAN SOBHAN

Agrarian Reform and Social Transformation

Preconditions for Development

ZED BOOKS

London & New Jersey

Agrarian Reform and Social Transformation
was first published by Zed Books Ltd, 57 Caledonian Road,
London N1 9BU and 165 First Avenue, Atlantic Highlands,
New Jersey 07716, USA; and in South Asia by the University Press Ltd,
114 Motijheel Commercial Area, PO Box 2611,
Dhaka 2, in 1993

Cover designed by Andrew Corbett

Typeset by EMS Photosetters, Thorpe Bay, Essex
Printed and bound in the United Kingdom by
Biddles Ltd, Guildford and King's Lynn

A catalogue record for this book is available
from the British Library
US CIP is available from the Library of Congress

ISBN 1 85649 169 2 Hb
TP   ISBN 1 85649 170 6 Pb

Contents

1. **Introduction**   1
   The early promise of agrarian reform   1
   Its subsequent devaluation   2
   The argument of this study   4
      The nature of agrarian reform
      The impact
      The rationale
      The political economy of agrarian reform
   Problems associated with this study   5

2. **Varieties of Agrarian Reform**   7
   Social origins   7
   Outcomes   12
   Processes of agrarian transition   13
      Latin America
      Asia
   A conceptualization of the nature of agrarian reform   16
   Radical and non-egalitarian reforms: the difference   18
   Agrarian reforms without social transition   19

3. **Selected Experiences of Radical Agrarian Reform**   21
   Social upheavals leading to egalitarian land distribution and social
      transition   22
      External intervention and social transformation: The Chinese case
      Radical agrarian reform in Vietnam
      Peasant mobilization and agrarian transformation
   External domination and agrarian reform   26
      North Korea
      Cuba
   External presence and agrarian reform   29
      South Korea and Taiwan: the Japanese impact
   Egalitarian agrarian reforms in Ethiopia   32

4. **Non-Egalitarian Agrarian Reforms Effecting a Social Transition** 35
   The Latin American experience of peasant mobilization   35
      Mexico

Bolivia
Nicaragua
Peru: transformation from above
Lessons from agrarian reformism in Latin America   41
Eradicating feudalism in the Middle East   41
   Egypt: perpetuating differentiation
   Iraq: a capitalist road?
   Syria
Decolonization as a road to agrarian reform   46
   Algeria, Mozambique and Angola

5. Non-Egalitarian Agrarian Reforms without a Social Transition   49
Redistribution without a social transition in Latin America   49
   Chile
   Land reform without land redistribution elsewhere
Agrarian reform within the capitalist mode of production:
  Central America   52
   Undoing agrarian reform through external intervention:
   Guatemala
   Honduras
   Panama
Social systems in transition: agrarian reform in South Asia   56
   Old landlords for new: the case of Bangladesh
   Share-cropping: its persistence in the post-reform phase
   Transition to capitalism within a feudal mode: Pakistan
   Elimination of capitalist relations of production? Sri Lanka
   India: transition to capitalist agriculture?
   South Asia: a system in transition
South-East Asia: the transition to peasant capitalism   66
   The Philippines: social transitions and persistent differentiation
Monsoon Asia: comparisons and contrasts in agrarian transition 71
Africa: decolonization and agrarian reform within a capitalist mode   72
   Kenya: building a capitalist agriculture
   Zimbabwe: a not dissimilar path?
   Tunisia: contradictions
   Decolonization and class formation: the dilemma of agrarian
     reform in Africa

6. The Economic Impact of Agrarian Reform   76
Conceptual issues   76
Problems of estimating the economic impact of reforms   76
The causal link between agrarian reforms and economic change   78
Agricultural policies and the economic impact of agrarian reforms   80
Agrarian reform in the context of a bias against agriculture   80
The contrary case   83
**The economic impact of radical agrarian reform in egalitarian
economies   83**

Policies to support the post-reform agricultural sector   86
Agricultural production trends   86
Equitable access to public resources   88
Structural changes in the economy   89
Diversification of the rural sector   89
The Ethiopian exception   92
**The economic impact of agrarian reform in non-egalitarian
  economies**   93
Farm management performance   93
Agricultural output   95
Agrarian reform and the improvement of agricultural production   97
Inequitable growth: the Mexican experience   99
The persistence of rural differentiation   100
The different impact of radical and non-egalitarian reforms on
  rural differentiation   101

7. **The Rationale for Agrarian Reform Today**   103
Trends in rural landlessness   103
Rural poverty   104
Demographic pressures   104
Rural under-employment   105
Rural wage trends   108
New technology in agriculture   108
The scope for labour absorption outside agriculture   109
Target group programmes for eradicating poverty   113
The case for agrarian reform   114
  *Relative productivity and the structure of production in relation
    to size of holdings*
  Capturing economies of scale following land reform
  The question of the marketable surplus
  Diffusing improved technology
Institutions and policies to enhance the efficiency of agrarian
  reforms   123

8. **Conclusion: The Political Economy of Agrarian Reform**   126
The scope for reform   126
The availability of land for distribution   126
  Latin America
  Africa
  The Middle East
  Asia
The scope for tenancy reforms   131
Preconditions for further land reform   132
Political feasibility   132
The future for agrarian reform   136
Reformism rather than agrarian reform?   137

Bibliography   139

Index   144

List of Tables

1. The Redistributive Impact of Agrarian Reform   8
2. Agrarian Reform and Rural Poverty   23
3. Land Availability, Rural Underemployment and Real Wages   106
4. Structure of the Economy, Growth in Production and Cereal
   Imports in Agrarian Reform Countries   120

To my son, Zafar

1. Introduction

The early promise of agrarian reform

In the first flush of the post-colonial era agrarian reform brooked large on the agendas of many reform-minded leaders of the anti-colonial struggle. The juxtaposition of an affluent class of native landowners, patronized by the colonial masters, with the grinding poverty of the rural masses, associated land reform with both decolonization and development.

The reformist compulsions of the emerging post-colonial elite were on occasion, however, invested with a sense of urgency by a rather different tradition of agrarian reform originating in the mobilization of the peasantry to seize land through armed struggle. This tradition spans the *Jacqueries* of pre-revolutionary France, Tsarist Russia, pre-revolutionary China and the innumerable peasant revolts in British India from the Moplah rebellion to the Indigo Revolt, and extends to the peasant revolutions led by the Communists in China and Vietnam. Their very different points of departure from the reformist tradition of agrarian reform lie in the fact that they originated within the peasantry which in the process came to challenge the prevailing balance of power in the rural areas, and even the state itself. The spectre of such peasant-driven movements for agrarian reform spurred on the post-colonial agrarian reformers to realize their own reforms without disturbing the foundations of the post-colonial state.

In the post-colonial era agrarian reform was seen by both reformists and revolutionaries as one of the levers to modernization and structural change of their 'backward' societies. Reform was thus seen as an important element in the goal of eradicating rural poverty. The reformers who sought to realize a move towards the capitalist mode of production saw agrarian reform as an instrument for increasing the incentive of the peasants to work their land more intensively in order both to enrich themselves and to generate surpluses to underwrite the industrialization process. The revolutionaries sought the destruction of a landed elite which was identified as the ruling class of the *ancien régime*. Both movements saw agrarian reform as a growth-oriented intervention which would lay the foundations of the new capitalist, or alternatively socialist, order needed to transform these traditional societies into modern developmentalist states. In the post-colonial era, the international aid agencies also embraced this logic and inscribed agrarian reform as part of their agenda for development of the Third World. Most textbooks in the infant industry of development studies articulated the logic of agrarian reform.

Debate has persisted over the form and extent of such reforms. The earlier European tradition associated with the enclosure movement in England sought to develop a capitalist agriculture to replace uneconomic peasant-based agriculture. The Soviet tradition associated with Preobrazhensky, on the other hand, sought to replace the post-reform minifundist agriculture with large capital-intensive collective farms. But the immediate goal of all reformers remained land for the peasant.

The compulsion for agrarian reform was obviously more than a slogan. In most parts of the developing world, from Latin America to the Middle East and South and East Asia, agrarian reforms of varying scope were carried through, sometimes as part of a revolutionary upsurge, sometimes by a high-minded post-colonial educated elite, sometimes by nationalistic military juntas, sometimes by the lower echelons of the landowning classes. The compulsions and circumstances varied widely and thereby conditioned the character, dimensions and outcome of the reforms.

Its subsequent devaluation

As we enter the fourth decade of the post-colonial era we find that, notwithstanding the noble aspiration of our founding fathers to vest land rights in the peasantry, there are today perhaps as many if not more people in the developing world living in want of land. Most of these classes of the rural poor are either totally dispossessed wage-labourers or poor peasants scratching a subsistence from micro or minifundist holdings whilst selling their labour to bigger landowners in a relationship which Alain de Janvry has defined as functional dualism, to compensate for the insufficient subsistence provided by their inadequate holdings (de Janvry, 1981). Thus rural poverty persists as the handmaiden of land poverty. Today the numbers of the Third World's rural population living in conditions of absolute poverty and relative deprivation remain as affronts to the conscience of a global community which has flown to the stratosphere, developed the nuclear bomb as well as the micro-chip, and eradicated hunger from most of Europe and North America. That we cannot eradicate poverty in most of the Third World has been seen as a systemic failure by both the left as well as by proponents of the market economy.

The apparent failure, whether in conception or realization, of an earlier generation of agrarian reforms to eliminate poverty and transform the rural economy of most developing countries had led to growing disenchantment with the promise of such reforms. The apparent failure of post-reform collectivist solutions to the land question in the former Soviet Union and Eastern Europe to build a dynamic agricultural economy has eroded the radical promise of such reforms. The spectacle of decollectivization in most socialist countries, the reversal towards household tenures in China and

Vietnam and now the dismantling of the collectivist system itself in Eastern Europe have undermined the verities which once underwrote the zeal of the earlier agrarian reformers. Those who persist with their faith in reform tend to advocate it primarily on grounds of factor use efficiency, appropriate technology and liberal democratic politics whereas collective ownership tenures are placed in the same pantheon of devalued institutions as feudalism and tribalism.

In such circumstances it is not surprising that few Third World governments, or even radical opposition political parties, place agrarian reform high on their policy agendas. Multilateral agencies, once in the vanguard of the intellectual movement for land reform, now mention such proposals for reform not at all or in highly qualified small print on the penultimate pages of their reports. Scholars who once staked their reputations on the need for agrarian reform have moved on to advocate targeting development at the poor, or to more fashionable issues of gender and sustainable development. Votaries of agrarian reform have been reduced to a fringe group of romantic throwbacks left over from the 1950s and 60s.

It is thus hardly surprising that in the last two decades we have witnessed agrarian reform of any significance in only a handful of countries and, there too, its outcome has done little to refurbish the image of reform. Indeed today, when there is talk of agrarian reform, it relates to introducing capitalism in the countryside of Eastern Europe, or decollectivizing the Chinese rural economy. The approach towards agrarian reform has typically become a casualty of the fallacy where failures in some countries have been transposed into a systemic failure of the whole agrarian reform agenda. The failings of collectivist agriculture in the USSR or of nationalized agriculture in Peru have overridden the transformation in the conditions of life associated with the end of serfdom in Eastern Europe, the radical land reforms of post-revolutionary China, Vietnam, North and South Korea, Taiwan and Japan which ended landlordism whilst distributing land and hope to millions of the rural poor. The hopes engendered by the Egyptian, Mexican, Bolivian, Chilean, Nicaraguan or Ethiopian agrarian reforms in eliminating feudal oligarchies have been subsumed in the pervasive persistence of rural landlessness, poverty and/or agricultural stagnation in most of the Third World. The focus, whether in the groves of academe, 1818 H Street in Washington DC, or even the FAO, is now on the diffusion of technology, integrated rural development, targeted works programmes and export-led industrialization. The fact that much of the Third World is still riddled with poverty, has lived through the last two decades in a state of economic stagnation, structural atrophy, collapsing agricultural prices and incomes leading to growing deprivation has introduced no rethinking about the weaknesses of the current anti-poverty strategies and the usefulness of a second look at the logic of agrarian reform. The need to distinguish between failures of conception and realization of the original agrarian reform agendas and the possibility of reappraising such reforms as an instrument for modernization, technological diffusion, development and democracy as part of a sustained assault on rural poverty have attracted little more than academic attention.

The argument of this study

This volume is thus directed towards making a modest contribution towards refocusing the development agenda on agrarian reform. The study argues that it is only those very few developing countries that have achieved reform sufficiently radical and egalitarian to eradicate effectively conditions of social differentiation in the countryside which have made headway in achieving sustained economic growth, as well as rapid industrialization, and have thus made the greatest advances in eliminating both endemic hunger and relative deprivation.

Our study seeks to sustain this argument by reviewing the origins, characteristics and outcome of agrarian reforms in 36 countries across the world so as to distinguish between failures of conception and failures in implementation in various reform programmes. It argues that agrarian reforms originate in a change in the balance of power in society and that the nature of this adjustment in relations of power has a profound effect on the outcome of the reforms. This argument applies to countries with quite different social structures and political trajectories – such as China on the one hand and Japan, South Korea and Taiwan on the other. The argument measures the wider socio-economic impact of reforms in relation to their capacity comprehensively to redistribute land to the land-poor. The accomplishment of such reforms will have to be examined in relation to their capacity to erode the power of the dominant classes in rural society and to arrest the process of differentiation which ensures the reproduction of a dominant class. The elimination of rural differentiation through a radical agrarian reform is thus seen to be central to the elimination of rural poverty, a wider diffusion of new technology, optimal utilization of domestic resources, both human and natural, and the development of the domestic market.

This study on agrarian reform is structured around the following issues:

(i)   the nature of agrarian reform;
(ii) the impact of agrarian reform;
(iii) the current rationale for agrarian reform;
(iv) the political economy of future agrarian reform.

The nature of agrarian reform

In discussing the nature of agrarian reforms an attempt is made in Chapter 2 to develop a conceptual framework which analyses agrarian reforms in relation to their socio-political origins, the corresponding change in the domestic balance of power and the outcome of the reform in relation to its impact on the process of social transition and differentiation within rural society. Using this conceptual framework for developing our typologies of agrarian reform in Chapter 2, we examine in the three chapters that follow, the historical experience of 36 countries which have carried out agrarian reform. This historical discussion is designed to give some appreciation of the variety of such reforms and the nuances which differentiate historical experience within particular typologies.

The impact
In Chaper 6 we analyse the causal link between agrarian reforms and their relation to agricultural development. Again, by reviewing the specific experiences of countries enacting agrarian reforms, we see whether there is any link between the nature of the reform as conceptualized in Chapter 2 and the performance of the agricultural sector.

The rationale
In Chapter 7 we discuss the rationale for a renewed emphasis on agrarian reform in the light of our review of the experience with agrarian reform in Chapters 3 to 6. The trends in rural landlessness, under-employment and growth in poverty are reviewed in those countries which have carried out land reform. The capacity of these economies to realize structural diversification and the development of alternative sources of employment outside agriculture and their implications for real wages are discussed. The efficacy of development programmes and institutions targeted on the poor and the incapacity of such programmes to arrest the growth of poverty is discussed in relation to the nature, extent and outcome of the earlier agrarian reforms. The case for a new round of more ambitious reforms is discussed in relation to the impact of agrarian reforms on economies of scale, diffusion of technology, the generation of a marketable surplus and the development of the market for the non-agricultural sector.

The political economy of agrarian reform
A review of the scope for initiating agrarian reforms in developing countries in contemporary circumstances would need to identify the domestic constituency for such reforms, the political forces aligned against them and the scope for new political coalitions being put together in their favour. The issue of whether agrarian reforms can be implemented outside a broader societal transformation in the internal balance of power needs to be reviewed along with the prospects of such changes emerging in particular contexts. The scope for societal change and agrarian reform may be examined in terms of the social and political pressures contributing towards change or currently promoting stability in particular countries. These are the issues raised in the concluding chapter.

Problems associated with this study

A review of the entire debate associated with agrarian reform and relating this to the contemporary experience of such reforms must suffer from its ambitious nature and the limited resources to sustain such ambitions. Such a task, if it were to do justice to the width of its canvas, would involve a full team of researchers working within an agreed conceptual framework for as long as it takes to capture the varying circumstances and experience of the agrarian reform countries across the globe. To attempt this task within the limited time and with the resources available in this study makes it inevitable that arguments will sometimes be over-simplified and important aspects of the problem occasionally omitted, perhaps even misinterpreted. The study is, however, designed to provoke debate on the need for further reforms as a precondition for realizing a transformation in the lives of the poor and will thus gain much from having its information base improved and its interpretations of social processes refined.

2. Varieties of Agrarian Reform

Social origins

The varieties of agrarian reform have been listed in Table 1 according to their social origins and outcome. The reforms are divided between those which originated in social upheaval effecting a transformation in the balance of power within the rural community and in society at large, and those which came about without any change in the domestic power balance. Such broad categories, however, need to be refined into a number of sub-categories if the full diversity of agrarian reform is to be captured.

If we focus on reforms originating in social upheavals, it is apparent that not all such reforms have originated in a popular mobilization based in the peasantry. Some reforms, such as those in Japan, Taiwan and South Korea, were legislated from above. Such reforms have in common with reforms originating in popular mobilization, a transformation in the balance of power capable of effecting a comprehensive redistribution of access to land. We have further sub-divided this process of social upheaval. One category relates to reforms which were stimulated by externally-induced transformations in the domestic balance of power. Such exogenous forces are identified as wars, invasions, colonization and decolonization. These upheavals are differentiated from upheavals which are derived from the internal dynamics of a society and usually associated with some form of popular upsurge involving poor peasants.

Agrarian reforms associated with a process of social transformation may be contrasted with reforms which leave the prevailing social order and power relationships largely undisturbed. Such reforms may be decreed by military regimes or they may be legislated by democratically elected assemblies. Some reforms, as for instance in Pakistan, may follow both routes at different points in time.

Our review has been based on the agrarian reform experiences of 36 countries since the end of the Second World War. This omits a few countries which have enacted reforms, but about which insufficient information is available; these include Myanmar, Cambodia, Laos and Afghanistan. We have included 20 countries from Asia, 14 from Latin America and four from Africa.

It is significant that few African countries figure in our list. This is because of the tribal nature of African societies in which title to land is deemed a 'gift of

Table 1
Redistributive Impact of Agrarian Reforms

	(1) % of Land Distributed to Total Agricultural Land	(2) % of Land Reform Beneficiaries to Total Agricultural Households	(3) Post-Reform Distribution of Land (Gini Coefficient)	(4) Landless/ Landpoor as % of Total Agricultural Households	(5) Social Transition Status
A. Radical Agrarian Reforms					
1. China	50 (1952)[4]	65 (1952)[3]	N.A.	Negligible	Feudalism to Socialism
2. North Vietnam	50 (1953)[4]	72 (1953)[3]	N.A.	Negligible	Feudalism/Capitalism to Socialism
3. North Korea	54 (1946)	N.A.	N.A.	Negligible	Feudalism/Capitalism to Socialism
4. Cuba	52 (1983)[3]	N.A.	N.A.	Negligible	Capitalism to Socialism
5. Japan	41 (1965)[4]	71 (1965)[3]	N.A.	N.A.	Feudalism to Peasant
6. South Korea	33 (1951)[4]	66 (1951)[3]	0.30 (1960)[1]	38[4]	Feudalism/Capitalism to Peasant
7. Taiwan	25 (1959)	29 (1965)[3]	N.A.	N.A.	Feudalism/Capitalism to Peasant
8. Ethiopia	N.A.	N.A.	0.43 (1977)[1]	N.A.	Feudalism to Peasant

B.	**Inegalitarian Reforms With Social Transition**				
9.	Mexico	43 (1970)[1]	66 (1970)[1]	0.938 (1970)	60† (1970)[1]	Feudalism/Capitalism to Capitalism/Peasant
10.	Bolivia	30 (1970)[1]	34 (1970)[1]	N.A.	85[2]	Feudalism/Capitalism to Capitalism/Peasant
11.	Chile	47 (1973)[1]	13 (1973)[1]	N.A.	53 (1973)[1]	Capitalism to Capitalism/Peasant/State
12.	Peru	37 (1976)[1]	37 (1976)[1]	N.A.	75[2]	Feudalism/Capitalism to Capitalism/Peasant/State
13.	Nicaragua	25 (1982)[2]	16 (1982)[2]	N.A.	32[5]	Capitalism to Capitalism/Peasant/State
14.	Egypt	15 (1987)[4]	10 (1986)[3]	N.A.	95[7]	Feudalism to Capitalism/Peasant
15.	Iraq	27 (1966)[4]	33 (1966)[3]	0.65 (1971)[1]	N.A.	Feudalism to Capitalism/Peasant/State
16.	Algeria	58 (1972)[4]	N.A.	0.72 (1973)[1]	N.A.	Capitalism to Peasant/State
17.	Syria	39 (1974)[5]	25 (1979)[4]	N.A.	N.A.	Feudalism/Capitalism to Capitalism/Peasant
18.	Mozambique	5 (1982)	Retained in State Sector	N.A.	N.A.	Capitalist/Tribal to State/Tribal
C.	**Inegalitarian Reforms Without Social Transition**				
19.	Tunisia	18 (1964)[4]	N.A.	N.A.	N.A.	Capitalism to Capitalism/Peasant/State
20.	Kenya	N.A.	3[3]	0.77 (1981)[1]	32[4]	Capitalism/Tribal to Capitalism/Tribal/Peasant

	(1) % of Land Distributed to Total Agricultural Land	(2) % of Land Reform Beneficiaries to Total Agricultural Households	(3) Post-Reform Distribution of Land (Gini Coefficient)	(4) Landless/ Landpoor as % of Total Agricultural Households	(5) Social Transition Status
21. Zimbabwe	18 (1984)[9]	N.A.	N.A.	N.A.	Capitalism/Tribal to Capitalism/Tribal/ Peasant
22. Bangladesh	Less than[11] 0.1	Less than[8] 0.1	0.60 (1983-84)[3]	78 (1981)[4]	Feudal to Feudal/ Capitalist/Peasant
23. India	1.5 (1986)[6]	2 (1981)[5]	0.62 (1977)[1]	55 (1980)[4]	Feudal to Feudal/ Capitalist/Peasant
24. Pakistan	3 (1972)[12]	2[10] (1972)	0.54 (1980)[1]	34 (1980)[4]	Feudal to Feudal/ Capitalist/Peasant
25. Sri Lanka	41 (1972)[7]	Retained in State Farms	0.62 (1982)[1]	43 (1980)	Feudal/Capitalist to Feudal/Capitalist/ Peasant/State
26. Indonesia	N.A.	29[6]††	0.53 (1973)[2]	66 (1971)[6]	Feudal/Capitalist to Feudal/Capitalist/ Peasant
27. Thailand	N.A.	N.A.	0.46 (1975-76)	13 (1978)[6]	Feudal/Capitalist to Feudal/Capitalist/ Peasant
28. Philippines	8.6[8]	16.8[7]	0.61 (1980)[2]	78 (1972)[6]	Feudal/Capitalist to Feudal/Capitalist/ Peasant
29. Costa Rica	2 (1980)[2]	3[2]**	0.83 (1973)[1]	64 (1981)[3]	Capitalist
30. El Salvador	15 (1982)[2]	15[2]	0.61 (1971)[1]	41 (1975)[4]	Capitalist to Capitalist/Peasant

	Column 1	Column 2	Column 3	Column 4	
31. Guatemala	16 (1954)†	N.A.	0.85 (1979)[1]	60 (1971)[4]	Capitalist
32. Honduras	4 (1981)[2]	14 (1981)[2]	0.78 (1974)[1]	41 (1970)[4]	Capitalist
33. Panama	15 (1970)[2]	12 (1970)[2]	0.78 (1971)[1]	N.A.	Capitalist
34. Ecuador	N.A.	N.A.	N.A.	75[2]	Feudal/Capitalist to Capitalist
35. Colombia	N.A.	10[1]*	0.86 (1970-71)[1]	66[2]	Feudal/Capitalist to Capitalist
36. Venezuela	6 (1973)[1]	35 (1973)[1]	0.92 (1971)[1]	40 (1973)[1]	Feudal/Capitalist to Capitalist/Peasant

Sources:

Column 1
1. World Bank, 1975.
2. Peek, 1986.
3. Brundenius, 1984.
4. King, 1977.
5. El Zoobi, 1984.
6. Haque and Sirchi, 1986.
7. Gunesinghe, 1982. This applies only to plantation land.
8. Sobhan, 1983.
9. Cliffe, 1986.
10. Tarp, 1985. This applies only to white settler land.
11. Siddiqui, 1980.
12. Qayyum, 1980.

Column 2
1. World Bank, 1978.
2. Peek, 1986, calculated for Nicaragua by taking work force of co-ops to total no. of workers in agriculture.
3. King, 1977.
4. El Zoobi, 1984.
*This applies to only those who are classed as in need of land and not all households.
**Applies only to Arbenz Reforms of 1954. This was returned to former owners.
5. Raju, 1986.
6. Huizer, 1972.
††This applies only to landless families.
7. Sobhan, 1983.
8. Siddiqui, 1980.
9. Qayyum, 1980.
10. Khan, 1981.

Column 3
1. Sobhan, 1986.
2. Hirashima and Muqtada, 1986.
3. Rahman et al, 1987.

Column 4
1. World Bank, 1978.
2. FAO, 1984.
3. Peek, 1985.
4. Sobhan, 1986.
5. de Janvry et al, 1986.
6. Hirashima and Muqtada, 1986.
7. King, 1977.

our ancestors' and vested in the tribe rather than the individual. Thus few who desired to till the land or exercise pasture rights on the land were denied it. This inherited right to the fruits of the land fell victim to colonial intervention which had a significant impact, in certain African countries, on the distribution in access to land and the dominant mode of production (King, 1977).

Outcomes

We have further argued that the outcome of an agrarian reform is related to its social origins. Thus our typology is constructed within a matrix which relates the origins of the reform to four relevant indicators.

The first estimates the extent of the reform measured by the proportion of agricultural land in a country which is appropriated for distribution and the proportion of agricultural households which benefit from this reform.

The second reviews the post-reform distribution of landownership as measured by the gini-coefficient for access to land – which is used as a distributive index. This measure, which is largely though not invariably derived from agricultural census data, does not always differentiate between owned and operated holdings. Since operated holdings take account both of land rented in and of land rented out, the traditional practice in a developing country is for the land-poor or landless to rent in land from land-surplus households to augment the size of their operational holdings. Thus there is a presumption that the distribution of operated holdings is on balance more equal than that for owned holdings. It must, however, be realized that in many countries minifundist holdings which have become too uneconomic to ensure subsistence for poor farmers are rented out to richer farmers and even to plantations or *haciendas*. It would, however, be rare for the leasing out of land by the land-poor to exceed in aggregate the extent of lands leased in or for the number of poor households leasing out land to exceed those leasing in land. Thus the presumption that the gini-coefficient for distribution of operated holdings is a possible underestimate of the actual title to land would appear to be valid.

The third measure of the outcome of a reform looks at the proportion of agricultural households which remain in the aftermath of the reform without any title to cultivable land. This measure is further refined to take note of the fact that a large number of households have over the years, under demographic pressures within the dynamics of a market system, faced a progressive erosion in the size of their holdings to the point at which it is insufficient to sustain their subsistence. To the extent that such situations prevail in a number of countries which have legislated agrarian reforms, we have added to our measure of landlessness the category of land-poor/minifundist agricultural households. This measure varies between regions. We have used a measure of one hectare for Asia and two hectares for Latin America and the Middle East to reflect differences in the potential productivity of the land. The common feature of this measure is the inability of holdings below this ceiling to ensure subsistence and its workforce's need to seek wage employment outside the household. This class thus merges with the landless to form the rural proletariat whose principal source of income is derived from selling its labour.

A final measure of the outcome of the reform is its capacity to transform relations of production within agriculture by effecting a transition from one mode of production to another. This exercise is logically derived from the attempt to trace the social origins of a reform to its social outcome. Thus a change in the social balance of power which precipitates a reform may be expected to impact on the dominant class which exercises power within the rural community.

Processes of agrarian transition

Having said this much, it must from the outset be recognized that the identification of a dominant class associated with a particular mode of production such as feudalism, capitalism, peasant agriculture or socialism, is fraught with serious difficulties both at the level of conceptualization and estimation. In very few developing societies can the dominant mode of production in agriculture be categorically identified. Presumably in socialist societies where there is, by definition, no differentiation in relation to access to the means of production, a clearly articulated mode of production is identifiable. In contemporary China, however, differentiations arising from differences both in labour power and skills located in a household and trends in differential access to some means of production are beginning to emerge. Such developments do not even enter into the debate on the nature of a socialist state associated with the writings of such Marxist theoreticians as Bettelheim (Bettelheim, 1968, 1976, 1978). To the extent that the means of production in a rural community remain collective property, as in Vietnam, North Korea, Cuba and China, the socialist mode remains clearly identifiable.

However if we look at other societies where a fundamental transformation in the social balance of power in agrarian society has been effected, as for example in Ethiopia, the virtual eradication of feudalism has not resulted in the emergence of a capitalist or socialist agrarian system (Rahmato, 1985). A number of such cases exist where either a class of landlords (defined as a class of people living off rent or crop shares derived from their ownership of the land) or a class of capitalist/*hacendados* (defined as people who both own and manage the production process on the land) have been ousted from their dominant position in the rural community. In their place a class of small and medium-sized farm households may co-exist with a large state sector which has taken over control of the plantations of the former landlords/capitalists. In such circumstances a definition of the dominant mode of production remains difficult since the prevailing system of production relations is clearly transitional.

This brings out the fact that the very exercise of identifying a clearly articulated dominant mode of production is difficult in the transitional stage.

These difficulties are aggravated by the problem of defining such concepts as feudalism and capitalism. Feudalism of the Middle Eastern or South Asian variety, based on retention of landownership rights with the landlord and the alienation of this land to the peasant for a share of the crop, leaves investment, management and production decisions with the tenant. This essentially economic relationship may, however, be mediated by a variety of non-market relationships which bind the tenant to the landlord and to some extent impose a reciprocal obligation on the landlord. Such ties may involve the delivery of various non-marketed services to the landlord or commitment to assist him in his factional/political and even physical conflicts. This in turn commits the landlord occasionally to mediate the tenant's relations with the state, provide rudimentary protection and occasional measures of welfare in times of economic adversity. Since such obligations tend to be specific to particular traditions, historical circumstances, ecological conditions and even to the individual landlord, it would hardly be feasible to enumerate or interpret this relationship within the limits of this book.

Latin America

The Latin American *hacienda*, whilst retaining many of the non-market linkages associated with the Asian model of feudalism, has its own distinctive features which makes the feudal order more akin to capitalism. Unlike in Asia, the *hacendado* was a direct actor in the agrarian economy. He managed his vast latifundia, marketed its output, operated in the factor market for capital and may even have been involved in commercial, financial and industrial enterprises outside the agricultural sector. The tenant/*colonato/peon/campesino* was tied to the *hacienda* through a system which has been appropriately defined as functional dualism (de Janvry, 1981) which denoted the involvement of the peasant household with both the capitalist and the peasant modes of production. Thus in exchange for a right to the usufruct of a plot of land on the *hacienda*, the peasant provided labour services on the lands managed by the *hacendado* at sub-market wages. He may be further tied to the *hacienda* as the market for his credit, output, inputs and non-agricultural consumption purchases. It would thus appear that whilst many of the non-market obligations of the Latin American *colonato* to the *hacendado* may be no less usurious than those of his Asian counterpart, his economic dependency on the *hacendado* appeared to be much more comprehensive.

The involvement of the *hacendados* in the rural factor and commodity markets and their entrepreneurial involvement with the land and even outside agriculture gave them the character of capitalist farmers. The move along this road from feudalism to capitalism in Latin America was thus a graduated progression rather than a quantum leap. The conversion of tenants who farmed their plots of land, not for a share of their own crop but for a share of their labour on the *hacendado*'s land, could much more easily be commoditized by conversion to wage payments.

Thus functional dualism of the contemporary variety in Latin America, where access to land on the *hacienda* is traded in return for paying below the market rate wages, is not that far from its origins in the pre-reform period of latifundias. Indeed, even where the tenant-at-will has become the minifundist owner of his plot of land after a land reform, the dynamics of the market still tie him to the *hacendado*, now capitalist farmer, due to the need to sell his labour to supplement the produce of his sub-marginal holding. This contemporary version of functional dualism which characterizes Latin American agrarian systems is thus not far removed from the pre-reform relations of production on the *haciendas* of the latifundists. Obviously there is a distinct cultural divide between the *hacendado* of the old order exercising his *droit de seigneur* and the modern sugar or coffee barons who live in the cities of Latin America with diversified investments in industry and banking. But the economic transition is not that great, and in no way comparable to the feudal order of the nawabs, rajahs and zamindars of the South Asian variety, for whom the very act of entrepreneurship in any form was a social defilement and who chose to invest their incomes from share-cropping in luxury consumption and patronising the arts.

The Latin American transition from feudalism to capitalism has thus been much more pronounced than that in Asia. What ambiguities exist in identifying the dominant mode of production arise in the treatment of systems where sizeable elements of subsistence agriculture survive in a post-reform regime. Here the definition of the appropriate relation of production based on the extent to which a household buys or sells labour, as distinct from working the land with family labour, suggests that capitalism is probably the dominant relation of production throughout Latin America (de Janvry, 1981). What we therefore have is a class of large capitalist farmers, corporate plantations, medium- and small capitalists hiring in labour for wages from the ranks of the landless and minifundist farmers. The 'pure peasant' is increasingly seen as an endangered species in Latin America.

Asia

This appears to imply a clear differentiation from the South, South-East or East Asian model where a large class of peasant households do survive, largely depending on family labour with some seasonal hiring of labour. This class co-exists with an indeterminate class of capitalist/feudal landowners who have in India been renamed as semi-feudals (Patnaik, 1976). This presumably means that whilst a class of rich and middle farmers continues to lease out its land to share-croppers, a growing number within this class now manage the land themselves with hired labour. To complicate matters further, they may manage part of their land and share-crop part, and may even occasionally practise this co-existence between modes of production on the same plot of land in different seasons. Amongst the middle peasantry the tendency to cultivate directly as much of its holding as possible with household labour, and to lease out on a crop-sharing basis any land surplus to household labour capacities, lends further ambiguities to establishing the point of transition from feudalism to capitalism. The tendency in turn of the sub-marginal household to lease out its land to a share-cropper and to migrate to the towns in search of wage employment makes the association of share-cropping as a measure of the feudal mode even more problematic.

The survival of a variety of non-marketed exchanges in Asian agriculture, even in contemporary times, mediated by ties of clan, kinship and those between patron and client ensure that the Asian societies are a long way from the conversion of all relationships between the owner and tiller of the land to purely market-determined ones.

We therefore suggest that our interpretation of the transitional process in our typology of the outcome of reforms be accepted as the reflection of a move along a path towards a particular mode rather than a definitive social transition.

A conceptualization of the nature of agrarian reform

We will not attempt to develop a model which tries to establish a causal relationship between the origins of an agrarian reform and its outcome. Such an exercise, which might lend itself to quantitative solution, may appear to be a challenging task to those with appropriate skills and adequate resources to invest in such an exercise. Here it would, however, be appropriate to establish a series of hypotheses tracing this causality which we will test out in a brief review of the historical experiences of some of the countries identified by us in Table 1.

The most self-evident hypothesis would appear to be that those societies which effected a fundamental transformation in the balance of power in rural society and in society as a whole could carry out comprehensive agrarian reforms. The measure of such a reform would be its capacity to bring within the compass of the reform all or a very large share of farm land and to redistribute this to all or a large proportion of agricultural households. The outcome of such reforms usually contributes to the virtual elimination of landlessness and ensures a highly egalitarian access to land. Such a social transformation frequently, though not invariably, leads to a transformation in the relations of production due to the complete eradication of the original dominant class.

Table 1 suggests that such a radical transformation was effected in those countries which are classified as socialist. These include China, Vietnam, North Korea and Cuba. However it may be noted that Japan, Taiwan and South Korea have also effected a similar eradication of feudalism which has been replaced by what we may best define as a peasant/capitalist mode of production. Whilst this mode is largely based on household labour, it is incorporated into a wider capitalist economy so that peasant households are integrated into the market economy. The radical agrarian reforms enacted by both socialists and East Asian capitalists thus share the same historical experience of effectively eradicating a feudal class and pre-empting the emergence of a new dominant class within the rural community.

The point of departure between the outcome of a revolutionary agrarian reform and one carried out from above appears to lie in the fact that in the latter equal title to land is not ensured after the reform runs its course. Even though non-socialist reforms can initially eradicate tenancy relationships and enforce a strict ceiling on the size of a post-reform holding, unequal access to other factors of production within households in a market economy could lead to considerable redistribution of land within the post-reform agricultural households. This could lead to the recurrence of functional dualism with unviable minifundist households seeking work outside the household. There could also be a revival of share tenancy relationships. Thus unless the working of the market in the sale of factors of production is institutionally constrained from operating in the agricultural community, as it was, at least until recently, in China and other socialist economies, even radical agrarian reforms of the East Asian variety can recreate differentiation within the peasantry in the same community. This differentiation will continue to operate within the limits set by a rigorously enforced land ceiling. It should, however, be borne in mind that the initial dynamism of a radical reform, even within the market system, if it ties in with a fast growing non-agricultural capitalist sector, can lead to a rapid increase in rural incomes even on minifundist holdings.

The state's need to generate an agricultural surplus from the post-reform sector to feed the non-agricultural sector encourages a regime of favourable policies to stimulate the farm sector. These may include cheap credit, favourable procurement prices, subsidized inputs and heavy investment in rural infrastructure. Thus access to public services and resources in a highly egalitarian landownership system which minimizes social, if not economic, differentiations tends to be more effectively diffused in the rural community. This may be contrasted with the tendency in other more differentiated post-reform societies where the unequal distribution of power in the local community influences access to yield-enhancing resources provided through the state or through the market mechanism, which in turn perpetuates new varieties of social and economic differentiation (Griffin, 1974). Thus an egalitarian agrarian reform, which at least eliminates disparities in local power, can be an effective instrument within a market economy where the government has a strong commitment and capability to support the agricultural sector.

However where the state discriminates against agriculture in its policy and allocative regimes and/or suffers from an insufficiency of resources to sustain its commitments, or faces failures in conception and execution of its policies, highly egalitarian reforms can contribute to stagnation in the expansion of productive forces. Thus poverty in minifundist holdings could be perpetuated rather than moderated as a consequence of radical reforms, albeit that this poverty is shared rather than located within a class of the relatively land-poor.

It would thus appear that whilst market forces may differentiate the longer-term distributive consequences of radical agrarian reforms which categorically transform relations of production on the land, both socialist and peasant/capitalist outcomes coalesce in creating conditions for the expansion of productive forces and eradication of poverty. This is because in both systems public services and resources dispensed under state policy can more easily be directly and equitably directed to the actual tillers of the land following the elimination of an intermediary class of power brokers. Growth of agriculture and increase in farm incomes thus becomes a direct function of investment in the farm sector and the macro-economic policies which define the terms on which resources are exchanged with the agricultural sector.

Radical and non-egalitarian reforms: the difference

Our typology thus argues that whilst the eradication of a landlord class could also be achieved without realizing egalitarian access to land, the operative point of departure from radical agrarian reforms thus appears to lie in the fact that non-egalitarian reforms leave a class of middle peasant/capitalists intact under the provision of the reforms, with sizeable retained holdings. This class retains the capacity to hire labour, generate surpluses and reinvest it in capitalizing its land; it remains equipped to absorb modern technology and within its resource base retains the capacity to benefit from technological advances and state investments in the agricultural sector. This class remains, both by virtue of its ownership of land and its ability to hire labour, a class apart from the poor peasant beneficiaries of agrarian reform. Fractions of this class may in some cases be drawn from the former landlord class operating from holdings within the retention limits of the agrarian reform. The socially differentiated character of this class gives it better access to the machinery and resources of the state and its capacity to exercise a mediatory role between the state and the poor peasants. In such a regime, therefore, the eradication of a feudal class merely transfers social power to another dominant class within the rural areas.

The outcome of an anti-feudal egalitarian agrarian reform thus differs from another which perpetuates differentiation in the countryside. Such reforms permit a higher level of inequality in their access to the post-reform lands and retain a sizeable landless class not accommodated within the original reform which under demographic and market forces may grow over time. Such reforms eventually lead to the replacement of the feudal class with a new dominant class of capitalist farmers, although the presence of a large state sector may dilute the authority of the incipient capitalist farmers and make them share power with a state bureaucracy which becomes an important element in the post-reform countryside.

Both the radical and the less egalitarian reforms, however, do have in common the assault on and eradication of feudalism as a mode of production. As we have seen, this elimination of feudalism derives from decisive shifts in the domestic balance of power due to erosion in the power of a dominant landowning class because of developments exogenous to the society and/or through the domestic mobilization of the peasantry. In our typology it is useful to differentiate between the specific historical forces which contributed to the reduction in the power of the landowning classes. It will be argued that where both exogenous forces and peasant mobilization interact this process tends to culminate in a full-scale social revolution leading to a transition to socialism, although such a transition may also occur due to the mobilization of domestic forces or where the outcome of the social transition appears uncertain. In societies where extraneous forces dominate the economy, however, a weakening of this external influence, which marginalizes the dominant class, could enable feudalism and class differentiation to be eradicated without a peasant mobilization.

Anti-feudal agrarian reforms, which have been derived purely from the internal dynamics of a society, may again take place through the medium of a peasant mobilization or through a top-down reform legislated by a class which is autonomous of the dominant feudal class. Such reforms, for different reasons, eliminate feudalism but retain the basis of differentiation within the agricultural community. It is obvious that any top-down reform which does not mobilize the peasantry in the articulation and implementation of the reform would retain the germs of differentiation.

However, peasant mobilizations may also become diluted in their intensity because they are themselves part of a coalition of forces rather than a peasant-dominated movement. Such mobilizations may protect the interests of a middle peasantry and thus leave intact sizeable differentiations in access to land. Such differentiations provide the basis for the growth of a capitalist class within the countryside.

Agrarian reforms without social transition

A third category of agrarian reform does not really effect a social transition within the agricultural community. Such reforms may disturb the relations of production only marginally, if at all. Redistribution of land may take place, but the differentiations within the agricultural community survive and may indeed be perpetuated. Some redistribution of power may take place within the dominant class where a more numerous subordinate fraction of the dominant class may displace the more narrowly-based upper echelons of this class. There may even be some redistribution of power in favour of the exploited classes but without disturbing the dominant class. In such communities a variety of modes of production may co-exist and the dominant mode itself may be difficult to establish.

The outcome of such reforms is usually to redistribute a much smaller proportion of aggregate land holdings to a much smaller proportion of agricultural households than non-egalitarian reforms which have effected a social transition by evicting a dominant class. Such reforms tend to leave holdings more inequitably distributed and a higher percentage of the agricultural community landless, largely because the redistributive compass of the reforms may be insufficient to benefit all members of a large class of landless or land-poor households. However where access to land within the given mode was initially more equitably distributed and/or such economies tend to be more dynamic than the economy with a more egalitarian agrarian reform, both landlessness and equity of access may be moderated by migration from agriculture to a fast-growing non-agricultural sector. The corresponding rise in real wages and improved access to land may even alleviate rural poverty.

Our classification of agrarian reforms as conceptualized above, which is discussed in the next chapter, has thus been broken down in Table 1 in terms of their origin and outcome as follows:

(i) Agrarian reforms originating in social upheavals which effect a social transition and eliminate social differentiation in the agricultural sector;

(ii) Agrarian reforms which effect a transition but leave scope for differentiation in the rural society;

(iii) Agrarian reforms which take place without realizing a social transition in the rural society.

3.   Selected Experiences of Radical Agrarian Reform

In this chapter and the two following, we will attempt briefly to analyse a number of historical episodes of agrarian reform within the framework of causality categorized above so as to give substance to the conceptualization of the reform process outlined in Chapter 2. This will enable us at the same time to capture some of the subtler shades of differentiation between the broader typologies of reform identified above.

This quantitative dimension of agrarian reform in 36 countries is summarized in Table 1, which makes a distinction between radical reforms, inegalitarian reforms which effected a social transition and inegalitarian reforms which did not achieve a social transformation in the countryside.

Table 1 attempts to capture the scope of the reform in terms of the proportion of the total agricultural land actually redistributed by the respective reforms and the proportion of rural households which were land reform beneficiaries, as defined by obtaining access to land under the reform. Table 1, of course, only looks at those land reform beneficiaries who achieved title to land, but the term also covers households which benefited from tenancy reforms, whether through enhanced security of tenure or a reduction in their crop-share or rent. Whilst tenant land reform beneficiaries are discussed in this chapter, Table 1 does not cover this group.

Table 1 establishes that, in terms of the amount of land redistributed in the reform, there was not much to choose between countries which effected a significant social transition but had widely different results in the degree of egalitarianism informing the respective reforms. In both cases from 20 to 50% of available land was redistributed. The distinguishing factor, with a few exceptions, was the percentage of land reform beneficiaries to total households. The radical reformers derived their title from the discernibly higher proportion of land reform beneficiary households to total rural households covered by their reform, compared to the inegalitarian reforms. In most cases the former benefited over 60% of rural households, while the latter, with one exception, did not extend their benefits to more than 40% of households. In contrast with both these groups, countries which aspired neither to egalitarianism nor social transition in their distributive regime reached, again with exceptions, a much smaller proportion of rural households. This may suggest that to realize a process of social transition the reform must reach out to a larger proportion of rural households and/or incorporate a high proportion of cultivated land within its compass. To realize both goals constitutes a radical reform. To distribute a high proportion of land is thus a necessary, but not sufficient, condition for a radical reform unless it captures a large proportion of rural households as its beneficiaries.

Even where the share of both land distributed and the land reform beneficiaries are relatively higher, however, the reforms may still be inegalitarian if the retention limits under the land reform ceiling are left high. The social outcome of the various agrarian reforms is thus captured in column 3 of Table 1 where we estimate the extent of inequality in ownership of land in the aftermath of the reform. Where such inequality in title to land is juxtaposed with the proportion of rural households left in a state of landlessness (Table 1, column 4) and poverty (Table 2), we capture the outcome of the agrarian reform.

A high of degree of landlessness co-existing with a high proportion of landless/land-poor households defines the inegalitarian character of a reform compared to those reforms which left few households without land and with existing holdings of land highly equitably distributed amongst landowners. Table 1 thus establishes the real dividing line between the radical and inegalitarian reformers as regards the compass and outcome of the reforms. The outcome is reported in Table 1 which looks at each country some years after the reform. However it should be noted that the data on coverage in Table 1 (columns 1 and 2) really looks at the impact of the reform in its immediate aftermath. The data in Table 1 thus establishes that only the radical reforms succeeded in eliminating differentiation within the countryside. In contrast, reforms which realized a significant social transition when enacted regressed into highly inegalitarian rural societies afflicted with considerable land poverty which left them in the course of time with social structures not dissimilar to those of countries which entertained no pretension to effecting a social transition through land reform. It is a telling comment on what constitutes a radical agrarian reform that the heirs of Pancho Villa and Emiliano Zapata in Mexico live in a rural social order not discernibly different from those which survived in the shadow of Somoza and the United Fruit Company in Central America.

Let us now look at the specific features of particularly agrarian reforms in order more fully to capture the nature of the radical and inegalitarian reforms, and their eventual outcomes.

Social upheavals leading to egalitarian land distribution and social transition

In Table 1 we list the following developing countries as falling within the above category: China, Vietnam, North Korea, Cuba, South Korea, Taiwan and Ethiopia.

Table 2
Agrarian Reform and Rural Poverty

	Country	% of Rural Population in Poverty		Distribution of Income (Gini Coefficient)	
1.	Bolivia	85			
2.	Colombia	54			
3.	Costa Rica	34			
4.	Cuba	N.A.		0.25	(1978)
5.	Chile	25			
6.	Guatemala	84	(25)		
7.	Honduras	80	(55)		
8.	El Salvador	76	(32)		
9.	Mexico	53			
10.	Nicaragua	80	(19)		
11.	Peru	68			
12.	Panama	67	(30)		
13.	Venezuela	36			
14.	Bangladesh	62	(1984)	0.36	(1985/86)
15.	India	51		0.38	(1970/71)
16.	Indonesia	47		0.42	(1981)
17.	Philippines	41		0.46	(1970/71)
18.	South Korea	11			
19.	Sri Lanka	26	(1980/81)	0.49	(1978/79)
20.	Pakistan	29			
21.	Thailand	34	(1975/76)		
22.	Kenya	55	(1980)		
23.	Tanzania	60	(1975)		
24.	Ethiopia	65			
25.	Egypt	25			
26.	Iraq	40			
27.	Syria	54	(1980/81)		

Sources:

1. Costa Rica, Guatemala, Honduras, El Salvador, Nicaragua, Panama (Peek, 1986). Figures in parentheses for these countries (FAO, 1987).
2. Colombia, Chile, Mexico, Peru, Venezuela (de Janvry *et al*, 1986). (These figures are for 1970, except Mexico which is for 1975.)
3. Syria (El Zoobi, 1984).
4. Sri Lanka (Hirashima and Muqtada, 1986, p. 18). (This is for 1980/81.)
5. All other countries (FAO, 1987).
6. Distribution of Income (Hirashima and Muqtada); except Cuba (Brundenius, 1984, p. 116). Bangladesh estimate for rural income (Rahman *et al.*, 1988).

The first four of these countries have experienced social revolutions, and not only overthrown the dominant class in the rural areas but have done this within the framework of a national revolution which has established socialism as the dominant mode of production. It is significant that all four social revolutions arose out of mobilizations against external domination; indeed, the social revolutions in China and Vietnam are distinguished by having emerged from prolonged armed struggles against foreign powers. A dominant external presence also had a decisive impact in effecting the balance of power in the agrarian societies of North Korea and Cuba.

External intervention and social transformation: the Chinese case

In the Chinese case, the Japanese invasion and occupation of the country fatally damaged the political legitimacy of the Kuomintang regime (Hinton, 1968; Wolf, 1969). The collaborationist role of the landed elite in China in the areas under Japanese occupation identified the fortunes of this class with Japan's military fortunes (Hinton, 1968). The vanguard role of the Chinese Communist Party under the leadership of Mao Zedong in the anti-Japanese war was of considerable importance in relating the outcome of the war to the balance of power in China. The anti-Japanese resistance made it possible for the Communists to transform their struggle against the feudal social order, which preceded the Japanese invasions of China, into a nationalist struggle mobilizing a much wider constituency. The techniques of peasant mobilization developed in the anti-landlord struggle of the Kiangsi Soviet became the basis of the anti-Japanese resistance. In their base area behind enemy lines in Yenan and other regions where the resistance had extended its authority, the Communists experimented with various forms of land reform, and this in no small measure helped to secure the support of the poor peasants for the Communist cause (Hinton, 1968). The explicit assault on the landed classes was moderated by the Communist Party as part of its coalition tactics with the Kuomintang regime and its desire to build a cross-class mobilization against the Japanese.

The relative success of the anti-Japanese resistance in the areas under Communist influence contrasted with the weakness, corruption and collaborationism of the social forces behind the Kuomintang, so that the defeat of the Japanese decisively tilted the balance of forces in post-war China in favour of a mobilized peasantry under the leadership of the Communist Party (Hinton, 1968). With the backing of a peasantry motivated by the prospects of agrarian reform, the downfall of the *ancien régime* acquired a certain inevitability. The victory of the revolutionary forces under Mao in 1949 meant that for the first time in Chinese history a regime which derived its power largely from the ranks of the poor peasantry had captured state power. This historic transformation in the balance of power in China was of decisive importance to the character of the subsequent agrarian reforms in the country.

Radical agrarian reform in Vietnam

In contrast to the Chinese experience, Vietnam had been exposed to a century of French colonial rule which had seriously undermined the authority of the feudal classes which had dominated the pre-colonial state. The French presence led to the introduction of capitalist relations of production into Vietnamese agriculture through investment by French *colons* in large plantations producing cash crops for the external market (Wolf, 1969). The landlord class still remained the dominant social force in the countryside, however, and production relations remained essentially feudal.

The surrender of the French in Indo-China to the Japanese in 1941 had a decisive impact on their authority in the region. Again it fell to the Communist Party, under the leadership of Ho Chi Minh, to lead the anti-Japanese resistance and effectively to seize power in 1945 in the northern province of Annam after the surrender of the Japanese (Wolf, 1969). The subsequent attempt to restore French imperial power in Indo-China, first with the assistance of the British and later by a French expeditionary force, led to the 30 years of armed struggle in Indo-China which ended with the military victory of the Communists in 1975. As in China, the techniques of peasant mobilization applied by the Communist Viet Minh, initially in the armed insurgency against France and subsequently against the successive regimes in South Vietnam underwritten by the United States, ensured the destruction of the landed classes first in the North and then in the South. Whilst the final demise of the landed classes of the southern states of Vietnam followed the end of the war in 1975, even during the insurgency against the French colonial forces landlords were being driven off the land and had to take refuge in the cities (Wolf, 1969). During the period of the anti-colonial war against France, the Viet Minh carried through a programme of rent reduction in areas vacated by landlords (Wolf, 1969). The landlords' authority was never effectively re-imposed, even where the South Vietnam government's mandate was supposedly restored in these areas after the 1954 Geneva accord. The subsequent attempts by various regimes in the South to carry out their own land reforms to counteract the influence of the Communists, whilst having a limited redistributive impact on the peasantry, further contributed to the erosion of the power of the landed classes in the rural areas of South Vietnam (Walinsky, 1977).

Peasant mobilization and agrarian transformation

The complete transformation in the relations of production in both China and Vietnam thus share the common historical experience of other socialist states where external events decisively weakened the authority of the landed classes through a disintegration in the authority of the state which protected this class. However, the two Asian revolutions had their own unique characteristics in that they drew upon poor peasants to provide the vanguard of their insurgencies and thus created a balance of power in the post-revolutionary state in which the concerns of this class would be given prominence in the councils of state. This gave a distinctive character to the Asian revolutions in comparison to agrarian revolutions where poor peasants were peripheral to the success of the revolution.

The vanguard role of the poor peasantry in the national liberation struggles of these countries meant that it emerged as the dominant force in the countryside after the success of the revolution, and agrarian reform in these countries was therefore carried through under the direction of poor peasants rather than an urban bureaucracy. In fact, the reforms followed direct action by the peasantry to carry through their own land reforms (Hinton, 1968; Chaliand, 1968). It is not surprising that, despite attempts by the Communist Party, especially in China, to moderate the impact of agrarian reform as part of its strategy of effecting a national democratic rather than a socialist revolution, the reforms were comprehensive. They not only eliminated the landlord class, in many cases physically, and abolished share tenancy, but sought to give all households access to land (Hinton, 1968). The result was the creation of minifundist holdings in many areas of both China and North Vietnam (Hinton, 1968; King, 1977). The diseconomies associated with the creation of a large mass of poor peasants with insufficient land to remain viable led both governments to the next stage of the reform, the collectivization of agriculture (Hinton, 1968; Min. of Agr., 1986). This aspect of the agrarian reform will be discussed in another context.

The outcome of the reforms in China and Vietnam was thus to effect a comprehensive redistribution of land, the elimination of landlessness and the realization of completely equal access to land. Such a radical agrarian reform eradicated feudalism and moved the agrarian system very rapidly from a peasant society of smallholder agriculture to collectivist forms of cultivation of the land.

External domination and agrarian reform

North Korea
The agrarian reforms in North Korea were no less egalitarian in their outcome than the Chinese and Vietnamese reforms and they effectively eradicated feudalism from the countryside. As in the case of the Chinese and Vietnamese revolutions, Japanese colonial domination of Korea meant that the landlord class had already experienced a drastic erosion in its feudal authority in the countryside. Indeed Japanese colonialism in Korea directly assumed control of the land and Japanese companies established capitalist farming enterprises which effectively transformed the feudal relations of production based on share-cropping of the lands of absentee landlords.

The Communist Party under the leadership of Kim Il Sung initiated armed resistance to the Japanese occupation; it is, however, not clear whether this involved the scale of peasant mobilization associated with the Chinese and Vietnamese revolutions. When the Japanese were defeated, the USSR and the United States moved to share power in Korea under the terms of the Yalta agreement, with their spheres of control being demarcated at the 38th parallel (Goulden, 1982). It was therefore Soviet control over North Korea after 1945 which enabled the transfer of power to the Communist Party which had led the anti-Japanese resistance in Korea (Goulden, 1982). The Communist Party of Korea, whilst having established its credibility in the anti-Japanese resistance, could not draw upon a mobilized peasantry with a history of agrarian reform during the period of armed struggle as was the case in China and Vietnam. The Communist regime in North Korea could, however, move immediately to confiscate the lands of the Japanese owners and to seize the lands of absentee Korean owners for distribution to the landless and poor peasants (King, 1977). The land reforms carried out in North Korea thus largely eliminated landlessness, realized a highly egalitarian distribution of land and eliminated feudalism.

Unlike China and Vietnam, however, the Japanese occupation of Korea had established capitalism in the countryside so that the erosion of feudal relations of production was already underway before the agrarian reforms. These reforms therefore faced little resistance from the traditional Korean feudal classes. The subsequent collectivization of the land in North Korea was also rendered easier than it was in China and Vietnam because the concept of working for wages in large capitalist holdings had already been established. As in China and Vietnam, when North Korea found the apparent diseconomies of minifundist agriculture a constraint on the expansion of productive forces and moved towards collectivization, the transition from peasant to collectivized farming was much more easily effected.

Cuba

The Cuban revolution was somewhat removed from the peasant revolutions of Asia discussed above. There was no direct colonial presence in Cuba, nor was there any episode of external aggression against which to mobilize the people during the course of the revolution, or an entrenched feudal oligarchy controlling the countryside. The Cuban revolution, led by Fidel Castro, was in fact a bourgeois-led insurgency directed against a long-entrenched, corrupt and repressive dictatorship (Wolf, 1969). The originally small-scale guerrilla war could eventually mobilize a wide class coalition of support. The support base of the Batista regime was, however, heavily dependent on a comprador capitalist class very closely linked to the United States' economic presence in Cuba. US capital dominated the trade, industry and agriculture of Cuba and relations of production in agriculture had been transformed by the presence of US capital. Investment by US and Cuban capitalists in sugar-cane, coffee and other cash crops, and also in livestock ranching, were closely integrated to the US market. A Cuban comprador bourgeoisie, rather than a landed oligarchy, was the support base of the Batista regime (Wolf, 1969).

The radicalization of the Cuban revolution arose out of the challenge to the hegemony of US capital over the Cuban economy arising from the need to expand productive forces and realize structural diversification of the island's economy in the post-revolutionary phase. This process was undoubtedly expedited by the political confrontation between Cuba and the United States. The assault on US capital thus emerged as the decisive factor in transforming production relations in Cuban agriculture (Wolf, 1969). The nationalization of US enterprises was extended to all large-scale capitalist enterprises across the economy. In the capitalist agricultural sector, where 28 large sugar companies controlled 20% and 40 large cattle ranches another 10% of farm land, this meant that altogether 37% of landholdings were incorporated into the state sector under the nationalization programmes, which had a decisive impact on relations of production and investment in agriculture (MacEwan, 1982). Rather than redistribute these large-scale capitalist holdings to smallholders, these holdings were directly converted into collective enterprises where the former workers were given a direct share in the management and profits of the enterprise. Thus the Cuban transition went directly from capitalism to socialism without an intervening redistributive land reform which could have created a large class of peasant cultivators.

Outside the capitalist sector the approach to agrarian reform was much more moderate than those effected under the socialist revolutions. Even though the reform was quite drastic, effectively expropriating 73% of agricultural land held in holdings above 402 hectares, this still left intact a class of middle peasants with holdings between 67 and 402 hectares, controlling 39% of the land. Another 8.5% of land was retained by 600 capitalist enterprises on grounds of their being 'particularly productive' (MacEwan, 1982). The second reform put a ceiling of 67 hectares on holdings, which effectively left an average arable area of 3.5 hectares per worker. This left around 160,000 small peasants with little or no capacity to hire in labour. This class co-existed with a state sector after the second round of reforms in 1963, when 76% of all agricultural holdings came to be held in the state sector (MacEwan, 1982). The transition to socialism as the dominant mode of production was thus a *fait accompli* in Cuba within four years of the revolution. To the extent that this transformation took place as part of a generalized assault on the Cuban capitalist class the preconditions for a socialist economy had been created in Cuba by the mid-1960s. Cuban agriculture thus came to be dominated by state farms employing for the most part the workers previously employed on the farms, who became the principal beneficiaries of the reform.

The Cuban experience demonstrates that external intervention reduces the self-reliance of an indigenous ruling class, and any diminution in the external presence inevitably reduces the power-base of an externally-linked local elite. The eventual overthrow of this externally-sustained class tends to be more easily realized even without resort to a protracted peasant-based armed struggle when the external domination of the economy has effectively been rolled back. It is significant that this external hegemonic presence over the agrarian system was part of a common historical background to all four socialist agrarian reforms.

External presence and agrarian reform

South Korea and Taiwan: the Japanese impact

The decisive impact of external hegemonic influences in transforming the domestic balance of power in agriculture is, of course, not limited to the four socialist countries discussed above. Redistributive agrarian reforms of a highly egalitarian nature took place in Japan, Taiwan and South Korea. In all three countries agrarian reforms of a highly egalitarian character were carried out in the wake of an externally-induced transformation in the balance of power. In all three countries Japan's military defeat in the Second World War and the presence of an external occupying power played the catalytic role. In the case of Japan, General Douglas MacArthur, the supreme commander of the occupying forces in post-war Japan, committed the United States to the destruction of the landlord class which it associated with the *ancien régime* that led Japan into the Second World War. The landed class was in no position to resist the directives of the occupying power and so accepted a very radical agrarian reform legislated by the Japanese Diet. This reform abolished share-cropping and redistributed 37% of arable land to 66% of all agricultural households (King, 1977). The compass of the reform virtually eradicated landlessness and share tenancy in Japan, ensured a highly equitable post-reform land distribution and provided, through a rigorously enforced ceiling, legislation against the emergence of a landlord class (King, 1977).

The defeat of Japan in the Second World War was equally decisive in the implementation of radical agrarian reforms in Taiwan and South Korea. In Taiwan, where Japan had been a colonial power since the Treaty of Shimoneki in 1895, the indigenous landed class had been effectively marginalized as Japanese companies took over large areas of land which were put under capitalist agriculture to supply the Japanese market (King, 1977). Some 21%* of the arable land was held by the Japanese on the eve of their surrender.

In South Korea, as in the case of North Korea discussed earlier, a Japanese corporate presence had acquired control over 16.7% of paddy land and had in the process transformed 26.8% of all farmers into landless peasants (King, 1977). As in the North, this Japanese involvement in Korean agriculture completely marginalized the social authority of the indigenous landlord class.

---

* Computed from (King, 1977, pp. 211–13) assuming that Japanese holdings, defined as public lands, came to 175,000 hectares and total arable land in Taiwan was 815,428 hectares in 1948.

As in Japan, the US occupying power in both Taiwan and South Korea used the vacuum created by the withdrawal of Japanese colonial power to push through land reforms. In the case of Taiwan the arrival of the Kuomintang government and army as refugees from their military defeat on the Chinese mainland by the Communist-led forces created a new source of power on the island without links to the Taiwanese landlord class or to the land. The Kuomintang were thus receptive to US advice to carry out a two-stage land reform which distributed 17% of arable land held by Taiwanese landowners to 30% of all rural households. Thus some 38% of arable land was distributed to 51% of all farm households. As in the case of Japan, this reform effectively displaced feudalism as the dominant mode of production, virtually eradicated tenancy and effected a highly equitable distribution of land amongst the peasantry. It is significant that an American land-reform adviser, Wolf Ladjensky, provided a common intellectual input to the reforms in both Japan and Taiwan (Walinsky, 1977).

As in the case of Japan and Taiwan, the US Military Government (USMG) in South Korea pushed through an agrarian reform which expropriated all Japanese-owned land and vested ownership rights on some 28% of South Korean farm households which had rented this land from Japanese landlords (Rhee, 1980). This reform effectively initiated the transition from Japanese-dominated capitalism/feudalism to a peasant mode of production. The USMG persuaded the South Korean government, installed by it under Syngman Rhee, to carry through this agrarian reform on property owned by Korean landlords. Even though the landlords were tainted with both subordination to, and collaboration with, the Japanese overlords, they retained some capacity to moderate the prospective agrarian reform laws being legislated by the South Korean National Assembly in March 1950. The new reform effectively vested ownership rights in share tenants, set a ceiling of around three hectares on non-tenanted land and moved to distribute all such lands above this ceiling to small and landless farmers.

There was some apprehension that this reform might be difficult to implement given the residual, if weakened, presence of the former landlords and their links with the local bureaucracy. This apprehension was put to rest by the outbreak of war between North and South Korea in June 1950. The subsequent incursion and occupation by the North Korean armies of the territories of South Korea led to the Communist regime carrying through a land reform in the South of no less radical dimensions than that it had earlier effected in the North. In the two and a half months before the US-led forces drove the North Korean army from the South, Communist cadres from the North had set up 18,000 farmers' committees in 1,189 out of 1,526 districts of South Korea. These committees confiscated 573,334 jungbo of land from the landlords and distributed it to 1.3 million, or 66%, of all farming households in South Korea; this reform involved 43.3% of the farm land of South Korea. Whilst this reform was promptly nullified once the North Koreans withdrew, it left a deep imprint on the consciousness of the South Korean peasantry and the concerns of the South Korean government and was a significant factor in pushing through a rapid implementation of the reforms legislated on the eve of the war.

The South Korean reforms had by 1952 distributed about 601,049 jungbo of land, some 29% of total farm land, to about one million families (Rhee, 1980). The land had been appropriated from 264,271 landlords, which indicates the radical nature of the reform and the low ceiling set by it. The social transition within South Korean agrarian society was thus from a class of small landlords marginalized by the Japanese occupation to an agrarian society of small peasants who effectively retained less that one hectare of land per household after the reforms.

Both feudalism and capitalism were effectively eradicated by the post-war reforms in Japan, Taiwan and South Korea, and the basis of a peasant agriculture was laid in these countries, with little scope for the revival of differentiation on the land, due to the limits set by the ceiling.

Whilst the debate persists over the precise definition of peasant agriculture or the peasant mode of production, the sense in which this concept is used in the course of this study relates to the cultivation by peasant households of holdings of a size which can be farmed predominantly with the use of family labour. This does not rule out the need for occasionally hiring labour for certain farming operations, but the largest proportion of the labour invested in the holding remains self-employed family labour. The main feature of this peasant agriculture in the East Asian context was that the small size of holdings ensured by the ownership ceiling set by their respective land reforms held out the prospect in both South Korea and, to a lesser extent, in Japan of perpetuating a minifundist agriculture which could neither promote the emergence of a class of surplus-producing farmers created by the dynamics of market forces nor eliminate rural poverty. Indeed, in both South Korea and Japan some differentiation within the post-reform peasantry and even some form of tenancy persisted. It was reported that between 1960 and 1976 tenancy prevailed *de facto* on between 13.5 and 17.6% of the agricultural land in South Korea, even though it was forbidden by law (King, 1977). This differentiation could not, however, lead to the emergence of a class of dynamic capitalist farmers largely employing wage labour or renting land because of the constraints imposed by the land ceilings. In these more regimented societies the clandestine evasion of land ceilings so common in South Asia did not provide the escape route needed to change relations of production on the land from a peasant to a capitalist mode.

In all three East Asian countries it was entirely due to the large-scale support of a peasant agriculture by the state that minifundist holdings did not perpetuate poverty and stagnation in agriculture. Furthermore, the dangers of demographic forces further fragmenting minifundist holdings and thus accentuating rural poverty was avoided through the rapid growth of the non-agricultural sector. The dynamism of this sector managed to absorb not just the surplus labour on the land but could even provide employment opportunities adjacent to agriculture so that a viable form of functional dualism could help minifundist farmers to mitigate under-employment and to augment further their household incomes through part-time work outside agriculture.

Egalitarian agrarian reforms in Ethiopia

The only country in Africa to have effected an agrarian reform of sufficient amplitude to transform relations of production on the land is Ethiopia. The military regime which overthrew Ethiopia's ancient monarchy in 1974 acted in response to increasingly violent public protests throughout the country in response to the conspicuous inability of the regime of Emperor Haile Selassie to cope with the famine which devasted Ethiopia in 1974 (Rahmato, 1985). There had been a tradition of peasant rebellion in Ethiopia, and in 1974 a series of peasant uprisings leading to occupation of land and seizure of the landed aristocracy's property threatened not only the Haile Selassie regime but also the social order which sustained it (Noggo, 1984).

The seizure of power by a committee of military officers, calling itself the Dergue, legislated its programme of land reforms in response to the growing militancy of the peasantry which was already changing production relations in the countryside through spontaneous local action. The Ethiopian agrarian reform of 1975 therefore reflected the concerns of an aroused peasantry (Noggo, 1984). Even though it was enacted by a class of petit-bourgeois officers and was to be implemented by sending some 50,000 students and other educated urban people to the countryside to mobilize the peasantry behind the reforms, the peasants themselves were in the vanguard of the move to eradicate feudal relations and in the process end all forms of differentiation in the countryside.

The reform bore the imprint of peasant militancy and was one of the most far-reaching pieces of legislation outside the Communist world. It abolished all private title to land, retaining ownership as the 'collective property of the people'. Land was, however, settled in usufruct on the actual tenant cultivators with a ceiling of 10 hectares per holding (Rahmato, 1985). Feudalism as a relation of production was effectively eradicated and the potential rise of capitalism in the post-reform countryside pre-empted by ensuring that the right to land would vest only with those who tilled the land.

Unlike many other agrarian reforms, the responsibility for executing the reforms was not left to the bureaucracy but vested in peasant associations based on existing villages or blocks of land of 800 hectares (Rahmato, 1985). These associations were to be drawn from the ranks of the landless, tenants and owners with holdings below 10 hectares. The associations were, unlike similar bodies elsewhere, for instance in Japan or in the Philippines, therefore made up entirely of potential beneficiaries of the reform.

In this respect the Ethiopian reform fell very much within the tradition of reforms carried out in China and Vietnam where the poor peasant played a dominant role. Given their particular social composition, the peasant associations used their mandate to bring about a rather drastic redistribution of expropriated excess land in order to give every member of the village community access to some land, even though some villagers received less than one quarter of a hectare (Rahmato, 1985). So, in contrast to most redistributive reforms outside the socialist world, where the appropriated surplus lands above the proclaimed ceiling form the quantitative limits to the programme of redistribution and thus limit the number of beneficiaries, the Ethiopian reform kept its distribution programme flexible, basing it on the need to give some land to all households within the association. This meant that the amount of land available defined the land retention ceiling rather than the number of beneficiaries.

A study of the implementation of the reform in four areas reported that after the reform in no area did holdings above five hectares remain (Rahmato, 1985). In one area the limit was three hectares, in another 2.5 hectares, and in one area, Bolloso, it was as low as 1.25 hectares. This meant that most holdings in these areas remained in the range of 0.5 to 1.5 hectares, though in Bolloso 94% of the post-reform holdings were below 0.5 hectare. This suggests that even fairly small farmers with holdings in the region of five to 10 hectares were being dispossessed in order to give access to land to all members of the village community. This indeed meant that, apart from the more complicated problems of effecting these reforms in areas subject to traditional tenure, in many areas large numbers of potentially sub-marginal holdings were being created. This of course led, as in China, Vietnam and North Korea, to the search for economies of scale to be provided through collective access to capital and even through joint production. This path was already being pursued in state farms set up to take over some of the large integrated capitalist estates. On available evidence it would however appear that the move to collective tenure was more rhetorical than real. A recent estimate suggests that in 1987 not more than 1.5% of agricultural land was being collectively farmed.

We will not pursue the many attendant problems associated with this drastic reform in Ethiopia. It did, however, effectively destroy all elements of a feudal mode of production in the country and did so without laying the base for the emergence of capitalist production relations. This was due to the initial mobilization of the peasantry as a precipitating factor in the Ethiopian revolution and its direct involvement in implementing the reform; the fact that the military regime was making an assault on both foreign and local capital in the urban sector ensured consistency in state policy. However the progressive nationalization of the non-agricultural private sector meant that a bureaucratic bourgeoisie was being built up and strengthened (Noggo, 1984). The perspectives of this new class were not necessarily harmonious with those of a militant peasantry. In the absence of a disciplined political party, informed by a coherent political ideology and with its own historical experience, no mechanism existed in Ethiopia under the Mengistu regime to integrate these two disparate elements within the Ethiopian state.

4. Non-Egalitarian Agrarian Reforms Effecting a Social Transition

The second category of reforms identified by us involves the overthrow of a dominant class and a transformation in relations of production, but leaves intact the basis of differentiation amongst the peasantry in the post-reform era. As indicated earlier, such reforms need to be distinguished between those which arose due to popular mobilizations and those which were legislated from above by military regimes. The countries to be reviewed in this context include four in Latin America (Mexico, Bolivia, Peru and Nicaragua), four in the Middle East (Egypt, Iraq, Syria and Algeria) and two in Africa (Mozambique and Angola). Significantly, no South or South-East Asian country appears to fall within this category. This may in part be because we have insufficient knowledge of the Myanmar experience and also due to certain problems of conceptualization of social transition in some Asian countries which we will discuss at the conclusion of this section.

The Latin American experience of peasant mobilization

Of the four Latin American countries included in this category, three (Mexico, Bolivia and Nicaragua) effected agrarian reforms in the wake of revolutionary upsurges, while in the case of Peru the reforms were legislated by a military regime. All four have, however, been fairly large-scale in their compass. In the case of Mexico and Bolivia they effectively eliminated the traditional landlord class as a social power, whilst in Peru a dominant landlord class and a modern capitalist class have experienced a significant reduction in their social authority and economic domination over the rural areas. In the case of Nicaragua, the social transition, whilst significant, has certain unique features which merit analysis.

Mexico
In the case of both Mexico and Bolivia agrarian reforms had their origins in violent peasant mobilizations (Warriner 1969; Wolf, 1969). The explicit target of these uprisings was the class of *hacendados* who exercised total control over the land and lives of the *colonatos* who worked the land for them in exchange for the right to cultivate small plots of land on the fringes of the *haciendas*. In

1910 in Mexico, 1% of the landowners controlled 97% of all agricultural land and 92% of the rural population were landless (King, 1977). These *hacendados* not only obtained the peons' labour for wages below the market level but bound them to life-long debt servitude through the use of credit and manipulation of the terms of trade resulting from their monopsony of produce from the peons' plots and domination of the sale of necessities to the peons. The *hacienda* was in fact a state within a state, and even police and magisterial powers were exercised by the *hacendado*.

The 1910 Mexican revolution, which originated in a mobilization against the dictatorship of Porforio Diaz, drew in the peasantry under the leadership of Emiliano Zapata and Pancho Villa who, through armed insurgency, began to seize the *hacendados*' estates (Wolf, 1969). The commitment to agrarian reform in 1915 by President Caranza was thus an attempt to diffuse the militancy of the peasant revolutionaries and win their support. However land seizures continued till Zapata's assassination in 1919, so that by 1920 the phase of peasant insurgency had exhausted itself with only a modicum of land being redistributed. In 1923, therefore, 13,000 landowners (2% of all proprietors) still owned 130 million hectares or 82% of all the land area, with an average size of 10,000 hectares per holding, while 59% of households with an average of three hectares owned 0.8% of the land.

The reforms initiated by a succession of presidents following Obregon in 1920–24 were therefore carried through to pre-empt future peasant militancy rather than in direct response to an insurgent peasantry. The reforms in their own right were one of the most comprehensive outside the socialist world, effectively distributing, between 1915–68, some 64 million hectares. By 1970, 43% of all farm land had been redistributed to 66% of all rural families. This major agrarian reform effectively eradicated the 'feudal' power of the *hacendados* and created the basis for a peasant agriculture.

The perpetuation of the peasant mode was, however, unique to Mexico amongst Latin American countries due to the institution of the *ejido* tenure system. This was supposed to be a return to pre-Spanish tenurial arrangements which vested title to land in the community. The community assigned the usufruct of the land to individual households which could pass it on to their heirs but could not sell or lease land. In 1970, some 43% of all farm land, 51% of crop land, was held in *ejidos* and 66% of the rural population were *ejidatarios* (World Bank, 1978).

Whilst the graduated nature of the Mexican agrarian reform, which effectively lasted 55 years between 1915 and 1970, was one of the most comprehensive in Latin America, its protracted character and the need to build a multi-class coalition to underwrite the Mexican state meant not only that the roots of peasant differentiation were never eradicated but that this differentiation was institutionalized to create the basis of a modernized capitalist agriculture. This class of rural capitalist had at its core the old *hacendados* operating within their post-reform retained holdings shorn of their feudal trappings. The very high land retention limits permitted by the reform reflects the inconclusive outcome of the Mexican peasant revolution and the capture of the revolution by a reformist middle-class leadership. Thus in 1970, despite a succession of such reforms, 10,000 agricultural holdings of over 1,000 hectares still owned 41.8 million hectares or 32% of all farm land. This reflected the concentration of ownership in the large livestock *haciendas*, so that only 12% of arable land was held in large holdings of over 1,000 hectares. But this still left title to land in Mexico highly unequal. The conventional measure of inequality, the gini coefficient,* for landholdings was 0.94 in 1970 (FAO, 1984); 48% of all farm families remain landless or land-poor, with holding of less than five hectares (World Bank, 1978).

Whilst this may be compared to the 98% of landless households in the pre-reform Mexico of 1910, the class of the land-poor had grown from 37% in 1940, at the conclusion of the large-scale land distribution of the Cardenas presidency, to 48% in 1960. Thus the impact of demographic forces on the dynamics of the market mechanism accentuated landlessness, notwithstanding the massive redistributions of land effected over 55 years of agrarian reform. Today landlessness is still a political issue in Mexico, though its implications relate as much to the inadequacy of the pace of structural change in the last three decades as to the limitations in the conception and scope of the land reforms. The end-product of this systemic failure in Mexico is challenging the legitimacy of the ruling PRI party and constitutes a threat to the stability of the Mexican state.

Bolivia

The Mexican experience has to some extent repeated itself in Bolivia where a feudal order rather similar to, and possibly even more exploitative than, the Mexican variant controlled the life of the peasantry. In exchange for small plots of inferior land and grazing rights for a few livestock the peasants had to work on the holdings of the landowners for between two and six days a week, usually without wages (King, 1977). In the highlands of Bolivia, however, 90% of the large landowners were absentee. In 1950, on the eve of the reform, 6% of landholdings of over 1,000 hectares, with an average size of 5,018 hectares, held 92% of the land, whilst 60% of holdings, under five hectares and with an average size of 1.4 hectares, held 0.2% of the land. As in Mexico, the Bolivian revolution in 1953 originated in an urban working-class uprising, but was joined by farm workers' unions which, under the momentum of the revolution, began seizing the *haciendas* and redistributing the lands amongst the tenants. This process continued between 1953 and 1955 before a radical land reform was legislated by the post-revolutionary regime. However, as in Mexico, the reform reflected the incomplete nature of the revolution and the capacity of middle-class reformists to dilute the radicalism of the peasantry. The reform not only permitted unusually high retention limits, but also provided a loophole for estates applying modern agricultural methods, which went up to 80 hectares of good quality land and 800 hectares in the highlands (King, 1977).

* This statistical measure indicates 1.0 as a measure of extreme inequality and 0.0 as a measure of complete equality as between two variables – for example, the total number of households in a country and the total amount of agricultural land or household income.

The target of the reform was the large *hacendados*, and in this respect, as in Mexico, feudalism was effectively destroyed. Some 9.8 million hectares or 30% of all farm land was redistributed amongst 66% of rural households. Indeed, if one focuses on cropland alone, by 1955 some 76% had been redistributed (World Bank, 1978). The social balance of power would undoubtedly appear to have been transformed in rural Bolivia as feudalism was effectively replaced by a widespread class of small landholders. However the nature of the reform permitted differentiations to persist so that in 1970 approximately 3,000 holdings, 1% of the total, still controlled 21 million hectares or 65% of all land. In some parts of Bolivia cattle ranches of over 50,000 hectares provide a measure of the growth of capitalist agriculture. Though again, as in Mexico, only 10% of cropland is held in holdings of over 1,000 hectares. In contrast it was estimated that in 1970, 57% of rural families were either landless or operating minifundist holdings of less than five hectares (World Bank, 1978). As in Mexico, the numbers of landless and land-poor households in Bolivia increased both absolutely and relatively, from 43% of all households in 1935, in the immediate aftermath of the agrarian reform, to 57% in 1970.

The Mexican and Bolivian reforms are classical cases of peasant revolutions which were originally no less powerful in their intensity than those revolutions discussed in the previous chapter, but which were diluted by their eventual loss of leadership to a reformist middle class. These Latin American revolutions effectively transformed the balance of power in the rural areas but not in the state. This retention of state power by a middle class created the conditions for the building of a capitalist agriculture which could co-exist with the minifundist holdings in a relation of functional dualism (de Janvry, 1981). The joint pressures of demography and the market tend to marginalize a progressively larger number of households, which are forced to seek employment in the capitalist sector. Even within the Mexican *ejido*, the only institutional mechanism designed to preserve the peasant mode of production in Latin America, a larger number of households are not only working for wages on land other than their own, but are clandestinely leasing out their land to adjacent capitalist farms (de Janvry, 1981). The system's inability to effect a sufficiently egalitarian agrarian reform has thus created the conditions for the perpetuation of agrarian differentiation.

Nicaragua

The third reform in Latin American originating in a peasant mobilization was the Nicaraguan revolution which overthrew the long-established dictatorship of the Somoza family. The Nicaraguan revolution, though drawing heavily on the support of the *campesinos*, was directed less against a class than a family oligarchy (Peek, 1986). Feudalism in the traditional sense associated with the non-market exchanges of Bolivia, Mexico and Peru was much less in evidence in Nicaragua. A capitalist agriculture with a sizeable component of medium-sized farms cultivated cash crops and operated livestock ranches, hiring wage labour from landless and land-poor households which co-existed in a relation of functional dualism with the capitalist sector. Thus 44% of households, operating units of less than 7 hectares, occupied only 2% of the land, whilst 6% of households, operating holdings of over 140 hectares, occupied 63% of the land (Peek, 1986). In the middle some 30% of the land was held by a class of medium-sized farmers in holdings of between 35 and 140 hectares (Peek, 1986). It was thus evident that pre-revolutionary Nicaragua did not involve the extreme inequalities associated with other Latin American countries, and whilst capitalism was the dominant mode of production in Nicaragua, a class of medium-sized farms was an important fraction of this class.

The Sandinista-led revolution of 1979 in Nicaragua was thus targeted not so much against a landed oligarchy but against that of the Somoza family and its corrupt and oppressive rule which had strangled popular aspirations for nearly half a century (Black, 1981). The post-revolutionary agrarian reform was thus initially directed at the Somoza family and its close collaborators. Quite remarkably, this family controlled not only a large number of industrial, commercial and financial establishments but also 2,000 farms covering 700,000 hectares (Peek, 1986), some 43% of farm land in holdings of more than 350 hectares, 12.5% of all farm lands. These 2,000 farms were converted into state farms in order to preserve the economies of scale and integrated management presumed to be conducive to efficient operations. This large-scale extension of the state sector into agriculture, whilst not diluting the capitalist character of Nicaraguan agriculture, undoubtedly shifted the balance of power in the countryside away from the dominant capitalist class.

A more class-oriented agrarian reform was initiated by the Sandinistas in 1981 when all holdings above 350 hectares in the Pacific zone and 700 hectares elsewhere were to be expropriated, if 'idle or used deficiently' (Peek, 1986). Holdings of over 35 and 70 acres in either zone, which were share-cropped to small farmers, were also to be taken over. The aim of the reforms was clearly to eliminate idle latifundia and absentee landownership whilst preserving efficient capitalist farmers of virtually any size. By 1983, this reform netted the state 350,000 hectares, which was still only 50% of the holdings of the Somozistas. These holdings were also largely converted into state farms on the same rationale as was applied to the Somoza holdings. By 1983, 20.5% of the land was being farmed in state farms and another 4.7% of the land in production co-operatives. Thus only 15% of expropriated land, some 3.4% of all land, was distributed to about 25,000 smallholdings of less than seven hectares which, as we observed, accounted for 44% of households. In contrast some 1.47 million hectares, or 26.7% of all land, continued to be held in holdings of above 140 hectares. Another 30% of the land was held by the same class of middle farmers who remained untouched by the reforms. Thus even though the state sector had made inroads into the holdings of the large landowners, capitalism remained clearly the dominant mode of production.

This continued dominance of capitalist farms in the post-reform phase was to some extent moderated by a regime which aimed to provide credit, services and inputs at subsidized rates to small farmers and to give them some support against the monopoly of the trading intermediaries, through guaranteed purchase by the state at favourable prices. However such price support and subsidies could not have been without benefit to the capitalist farmers, as was evident from the fact that state credit to small farmers doubled between 1977 and 1981, so that in 1981 no less than 77.4% of the credit still went to large and medium farmers in rough proportion to their control of the land.

It might, however, be pointed out that, unlike the Mexican and Bolivian revolutions, the party leading the Nicaraguan revolution, the Sandinistas, explicitly claimed to be socialist in its orientation and depend on the *campesinos* as its principal base of political support. Nicaragua's growing confrontation with the United States and the impact of the Contra insurgency underwritten by the US served to polarize Nicaraguan society. The attempt to reconcile the contradictions between the peasantry and the capitalist class in the agricultural sector was pushing the Sandinistas towards a more radical strategy on the land. This, however, has been frustrated by the electoral defeat of the Sandinista regime by the party of President Chamorro which appears more conspicuously aligned to the privileged classes which supported the Somoza regime. There is, however, no indication that land seized by the state under the Sandinista regime is being returned to its previous owners.

Peru: transformation from above
The last of the agrarian transformations in Latin America which merit attention is the Peruvian agrarian reform carried out by a military regime between 1970 and 1976. The reform in Peru had by 1979 redistributed 37% of all crop and grazing land in the country to some 37% of rural families (Open University, 1983). This reform was designed to change the balance of power within the agrarian society of Peru away from a class of feudal landlords in the highlands and capitalist plantation owners in the coastal region. Whilst the reform may effectively have eliminated the social power of the *hacendados* of the highlands, it is less clear if capitalist relations of production have been effectively undermined, and in 1973 some 1,500 holdings still held 7.5 million hectares or 42% of the land. The target of the 1976 reform of reducing these holdings to 20% of all agricultural land was not fully realized and eventually about a third of these large holdings may be estimated to still be held in units of more than 1,000 hectares (Open University, 1983). This suggests that the loopholes in the ceiling legislation have permitted such holdings to survive.

The attempt by the Peruvian junta to arrest the growth of minifundist holdings by placing land in large collective/co-operative holdings is, however, more problematic in identifying the direction and dimension of the social transition effected by the reforms. The sugar plantations of the coast have effectively been converted into state enterprises, but the attempt to collectivize the tenanted *haciendas* of the highlands appears to have been successful only in collectivizing ownership whilst leaving the unit of production in the hands of the former tenant farmers; minifundist agriculture still appears to be pervasive in Peru (King, 1977).

The Peruvian reform has left a large number of landless rural households outside its compass. In 1975 it was estimated that 60% of rural households would remain in the category of landless or land-poor (those with less than five hectares) (World Bank, 1978). This differentiation appears to be built into the Peruvian agrarian system and the amplitude of the reform has not been sufficient to moderate this seriously. The Peruvian system thus represents an unstable co-existence between the majority of landless and land-poor households, a large state sector and an equally large class of capitalist farmers. The resolution of this unstable equilibrium was left unresolved by the Peruvian military whose attempt to effect reform from above without involving the peasants alienated all components of the polity and contributed to their unceremonious abdication of state power to civilian rule (Maniruzzaman, 1987). It remains to be seen how effectively the democratic regimes in Peru move to incorporate the landless and land-poor within a more equitable agrarian order. The fact that agrarian violence under the leadership of the Shining Path guerrilla insurgency movement continues to draw upon the disaffections of the peasantry suggests that the agrarian revolution in Peru remains incomplete.

Lessons from agrarian reformism in Latin America

The Latin American experience appears to have the common feature that each of the agrarian reforms has effected significant modifications in the balance of power within agrarian society. However in none of these societies was the reform of sufficient amplitude to realize an egalitarian redistribution of land remotely comparable with the reforms discussed in the previous chapter. The insufficiency of this redistribution has permitted differentiations within agriculture to persist. So, even though some form of social transition has been realized and elements of feudalism have been eradicated, the capitalist revolution remains far from complete and shows little signs of eradicating the minifundist agriculture which seems bound to it in a relation of functional dualism (de Janvry et al., 1986). In the case of Mexico, Bolivia and Peru, despite the degree of social upheaval, the end-product of their agrarian reforms appears to be a class of impoverished minifundist farmers and another of landless agricultural workers providing cheap labour on capitalist holdings which have become dominant throughout Latin America outside Cuba.

Eradicating feudalism in the Middle East

We have identified four countries in the Arab world where a fundamental change in the balance of power brought about an agrarian reform which effectively destroyed the authority of the dominant class in rural society. These countries are Egypt, Iraq, Syria and Algeria, and in this category one might also include Libya and South Yemen. In South Yemen a socialist regime is supposed to have eliminated the domination of tribal chiefs in the countryside (Halliday, 1974). Insufficient information on South Yemen has constrained us from analysing the agrarian transition in that country. Similarly in Libya, after the overthrow of the monarchy by a junta of military officers led by Colonel Gaddafy in 1968, land controlled by tribal sheiks was appropriated for distribution along with land seized from Italian settlers operating capitalist farms (Bearman, 1986). Insufficient information about this reform precludes fuller discussion of its impact.

The social transitions realized in Egypt, Iraq, Syria and Libya were brought about by military regimes rather than popular mobilization. In the case of Egypt, Iraq and Libya a group of mid-level officers, drawn largely from the petit-bourgeoisie, overthrew monarchies, sustained by a feudal class of big landlords, though in Libya the tribal chiefs were not quite in the same social category as the landlords of Egypt and Iraq (Abdel-Malek, 1968; Caracatus, 1959). The three monarchies were all identified with making their countries subservient to imperialist interests. Egypt and Iraq were seen as part of a British sphere of influence (Kimche, 1950), and Iraq was also tied into the Baghdad Pact fashioned by the United States, while Libya had provided bases for the US Air Force. The assault on the monarchies was thus explicitly anti-imperialist, designed to assert national sovereignty, so the attack on feudalism was a subsidiary objective resulting from the links between the ruling classes and the imperialist dominance over these countries.

In all three countries the assault on feudalism proved to be decisive and the class of feudal lords and tribal chiefs was effectively eliminated as a social force. In the post-reform phase, however, the ethos of the revolutions, derived again from the composition of the social forces contending for state power, has influenced the outcome of the agrarian reforms carried out under the anti-feudal revolution.

Egypt: perpetuating differentiation
In Egypt the officers who carried out the reform were sensitive to the inequities in the agrarian structure (Abdel-Malik, 1968). They had no class identification with the feudal classes which had traditionally dominated the countryside. This landed class was closely identified with the Egyptian monarchy which had been the immediate target of the military plotters, led by Colonel Gamal Abdul Nasser in 1952. In Egypt on the eve of the reform, 2,119 landowners, just 0.1% of rural landowners, holding over 200 acres of land, owned 20% of the land, whilst 72% of rural landowners farmed holdings of less than one acre, covering 13% of the land (King, 1977). Some 75% of this farmland was rented. These inequities were so extreme that even the long silent *fellahin* were moved to acts of violence against landholders. Gamal Nasser's military regime thus had a clearly defined political target and a ready constituency amongst most classes of the peasantry who were not close to the large landowners.

The agrarian reform set a high ceiling of around 100 acres with a variety of retention provisions which could further expand the size of the retained holdings. Thus the majority of middle and even fairly large landowners were left untouched by the reform. These reforms therefore left some 1.2% of households, with holdings of 20 acres and above, in control of 25% of the land in 1965 (King, 1977). Whilst much of this class was drawn from the ranks of the middle and rich peasantry, some was also drawn from the dispossessed landlords who operated lands which they held under the retention limits set by the agrarian reform.

Even though one-sixth of the cultivable land of Egypt was affected by the land reform of 1952 and redistributed by 1967 to 317,000 *fellahin*, about 10% of all farm owners, access to land remained polarized. A large class of subsistence farmers, defined as having holdings of less than five acres, accounted for 95% of farm owners and farmed 57% of the land. At the other end of the spectrum a class of capitalist farmers survived and prospered. They hired labour from the ranks of the large and growing number of landless rural proletariat left untouched by the land reforms and from the ranks of the small farmers whose holdings were insufficient to ensure their subsistence.

The eradication of feudalism in Egypt has indeed been realized by the agrarian reforms; the worst aspects of share tenancy agriculture and feudal oppression have been abolished and some of the landless and small farmers have received land and/or enhanced their holdings. It would, however, appear that a land reform legislated from above and implemented by the bureaucracy has been insufficient to cope with the hunger for land and employment or to eradicate rural poverty in the Egyptian countryside. It has, rather, permitted a new pattern of differentiation to persist and for a form of capitalism to become the established mode of production in the countryside. This new class can reproduce itself, growing in strength by exploiting the growing pool of labour drawn from the ranks of the landless and land-poor and from appropriation of lands through the lease and clandestine sale of small farmers' land. Many small farmers who had benefited from the land reform nevertheless find agriculture an uneconomic occupation and choose to seek their fortunes either in the towns or, in large numbers, in the oil-exporting countries of the Arab world.

Iraq: a capitalist road?

The pattern of differentiation and emergent capitalism in the countryside discernible in Egypt also characterized the outcome of the agrarian reforms in Iraq. Here too a group of army officers carried out a fairly far-reaching agrarian reform in two stages (in 1958 and 1970) directed to end a highly inegalitarian feudal order (Warriner, 1969). These inequalities were aggravated by the illegal appropriation by tribal leaders of tribal lands in the newly irrigated areas where the modernization of traditional agriculture became possible because of investment by the state in large water-control programmes. Thus 272 landowners had holdings of over 2,500 hectares and another 3,620 had holdings above 250 hectares (King, 1977). In contrast 89% of the peasants were landless. This feudal class in Iraq was closely identified with the monarchy so that the overthrow of the monarchist regime in 1958 by a group of army officers, again of petit-bourgeois origin and with few links to the feudal lords, found a ready target in this class of landlords and a basis for rallying the dispossessed peasantry.

By 1966 the redistributive land reform legislation in Iraq yielded around 1.4 million hectares of land, of which some 1.25 million hectares were requisitioned from 2,433 owners (King, 1977). However by 1968 only 650,000 acres were distributed, some of which was state land, to 300,000 dwellers.

The large area of land covered by the reform still left sizeable lands with the former landowners due to inordinately high retention limits set by the 1958 reform. This allowed 250 hectares of irrigated plus 500 hectares of rain-fed land as the personal ceiling, although this was lowered to 75 hectares of irrigated and 100 hectares of rain-fed land in 1970. These ceilings not only left intact a class of potentially big farmers but also permitted many former landowners to retain their land through various clandestine forms of sub-division.

As in Egypt, the feudal aspects of the relationship on the land appear to have been eradicated though aspects of feudalism appear to have persisted in parts of Iraq well after the reforms (Warriner, 1969). Some of the old feudal lords and the bigger farmers survived, however, to provide the basis for a fast-growing capitalist sector in the heart of an ostensibly 'socialist' Iraq. Ineffectual attempts to promote socialism in agriculture by setting up state farms and issuing top-down edicts to set up co-operatives in the reformed sector have done little to discourage the growth of this class.

The survival and growth of capitalism in Iraq has indeed provided an opening for members of the urban professional classes, as well as the country's bureaucratic, military and political elite to set up commercial farms directly or in partnership with this new class. This new class is now operating large farms, using capital-intensive techniques of production with access to subsidized inputs, state-supplied credit and, in recent years, the right to lease state lands at subsidized rentals (Springborg, 1986).

The overthrow of feudalism in Iraq, despite the ruling party's socialist rhetoric, therefore did little to eradicate differentiation in the countryside, make the reform beneficiaries economically viable or even to expand productive forces. The move towards capitalist agriculture, based on producing cash crops for the urban markets, has thus emerged as a logical outcome of the post-1958 agrarian reforms in Iraq.

The principal constraint on the emergence of capitalism as the dominant mode of production in Iraq will, however, remain the limited supply of cheap agricultural labour. The rural population of Iraq contracted from 49% in 1965 to 30% of the total population in 1985, whilst the agricultural sector fell from 50% to 30% of the total labour force in the same period (World Bank, 1987). The availability of abundant oil revenues for investment in development has given greater opportunity for the Iraqi small farmer to leave his uneconomic holding and seek work in urban areas, so Iraqi agriculture has already had to opt for more capital-intensive techniques which impose certain limits on the market viability of the capitalist mode of production.

Syria

As in Egypt and Iraq, until the 1958 agrarian reforms feudal relations of production were dominant in Syria where 70% of the rural population was landless and 75% of the land was cultivated under share tenancy (King, 1977). In contrast land held in estates of over 100 hectares occupied 52% of the land, and 10% of the land was in holdings of over 1,000 hectares (El-Zoobi, 1984).

The landlords reinforced their hold over the tenants through control of access to water, inputs, credit and the market for their products, making the relationship not dissimilar to that on the *haciendas* of pre-1910 Mexico. As in the Latin American system, under one form of tenure, *zameh*, the landlord assigned land to tenants on his land for personal cultivation in return for labour on the landlord's land. This suggested the emergence of a form of capitalist landowner who, whilst himself absentee, operated the land through managers. Such landowners were frequently part of the urban middle class who make commercial investments in land.

Unlike Egypt and Iraq, the Syrian landowners did not owe loyalty to the crown, as Syria was a republic under the French sphere of influence after the Sykes–Picot agreement at the end of the First World War (Kimche, 1950). The landlords and commercial bourgeoisie were the dominant force in the Syrian state. The assault on Syrian feudalism was in fact a consequence of the union with Egypt, effected in 1958, rather than dynamics within the Syrian polity (King, 1977).

The 1958 reform in Syria followed the Egyptian reform in fixing a ceiling per owner of 80 hectares of irrigated and 300 hectares of non-irrigated land. A further 40 hectares of irrigated and 160 hectares of non-irrigated land could be transferred to the landowner's family members. Various measures to regulate tenancy on slightly more favourable terms for the tenant were enacted. Under this reform the expropriable area was identified as 1.5 million hectares from the land of 3,240 large landowners. By 1961, however, 670,000 hectares had been expropriated and only 176,000 distributed in lots of eight hectares to about 15,000 families.

In 1963 a new land reform initiated under the leadership of the Baath Socialist Party further lowered the ceiling in regionally variable lots of 15–55 hectares for irrigated land, 35–40 hectares for orchard land and 80–300 hectares for rain-fed land. As a result a further 1,372 landowners surrendered 350,000 hectares. In 1980 a further reform marginally reduced ceilings to 15–45 hectares for irrigated land, 30–55 hectares for orchards and 85–140 hectares for rain-fed lands (El-Zoobi, 1984). By 1979 a total of 1.46 million hectares of land had been expropriated under the first two reforms, though only a small part of this was irrigated. During this period 574,093 hectares were distributed to 62,551 families or 331,734 individuals. Another 421,596 hectares of land under state domain was distributed to 38,219 families.

The agrarian reforms in Syria, as in Egypt and Iraq, were sufficiently far-reaching to eliminate the feudal power of the large landowners and tribal chiefs as a social force in the countryside. However high retention limits for land permitted the commercial landlord class to retain a dominant presence in the countryside. In 1970 some 30% of the land was held in units of over 50 hectares by 2.5% of the landowners, whilst 72% of landowners held minifundist holdings with an average size of 3.16 hectares, which was itself highly fragmented. The below-subsistence incomes generated by smallholdings thus had to be supplemented by wages earned on the farms of the capitalist landowners.

Syrian reforms were obviously insufficient to eliminate differentiation within the countryside and have, despite the socialist commitment by the ruling Baath Party, permitted capitalism to thrive in the countryside. Landless and land-poor households find their numbers augmented by the dynamics of the market, demography and inheritance laws. Syrian agriculture has not been able to trade off its lack of equity with a significant expansion in productive forces under the leadership of the capitalist farmers.

Decolonization as a road to agrarian reform

The three other states where a transformation in the relations of production have been effected are Algeria, Mozambique and Angola. These cases are discussed separately from the others in this chapter because they derive from the process of decolonization. Whilst a large number of Third World countries have experienced decolonization, only in a very few has the withdrawal of the colonial power had an immediate impact on the relations of production. This has taken place only in those countries where colonial rule introduced a settler population which did not merely co-exist with traditional tenures but established capitalism as the dominant mode of production in the agricultural sector. However it was only in those countries where the nature of the liberation struggle precipitated a sudden withdrawal of the settler population that capitalist relations of production came to be noticeably modified. The most important cases where this took place were in Algeria, Mozambique and Angola. In all three cases liberation came at the end of a bloody war after which the settlers felt sufficiently insecure in the face of a mobilized peasantry to abandon their farms and seek refuge in the mother country, thus leaving a visible entrepreneurial vacuum in the agricultural sector.

Algeria, Mozambique and Angola

In 1962 in Algeria, on the eve of independence from France, 21,674 French *colons* held one-third of the cultivable land and accounted for 60% of crop production. Within a year of independence the French settler population withdrew leaving behind 2.8 million hectares of land. The nationalization of these lands by the Algerian government thus took place to fill a vacuum with a view to maintaining pre-independence levels of production. The consequence of this intervention was to make the state into the largest single landowner in Algeria and to create the basis of a version of state capitalism/socialism/self-management (there is much confusion and controversy over precisely what kind of system it was) in the heart of the agricultural sector. This sector continued to co-exist with a private sector in agriculture characterized by visible inequalities in the distribution of cultivable land.

The dominance of French *colons* in Algeria, who controlled the most fertile lands, over the agricultural sector effectively pre-empted the growth of a feudal class or even a sizeable class of indigenous capitalists. Even though noticeable inequalities in non-*colon* agricultural lands persisted, landlessness was a major social problem and absentee landowners appropriated 10% of agricultural output as ground rent in the non-reform sector after the nationalization of *colon* land. It was evident that a landed elite, which effectively dominated rural life in Algeria, did not exist at the time of independence. The appropriation of *colon* lands in post-independence Algeria pre-empted the growth of a feudal or capitalist class with a capacity to dominate the lives of the poor and landless rural households.

A similar situation characterized the withdrawal of Portuguese colonialism from Southern Africa. In Mozambique, Portuguese settlers controlled much of the cultivable land and marketed farm output, and in Angola the settler presence was equally dominant. In both countries these configurations of colonial power prevented the emergence of a dominant indigenous class, or even a class of viable smallholders, as was the case in parts of West Africa. The sudden withdrawal of settler populations in these countries, as in Algeria, led to the expansion of the state sector, which became dominant, although it co-existed with various forms of household and tribal tenure. This expansion of the state sector was dictated by the need to keep intact the apparent economies of scale of large, integrated farms, but also reflected the socialist orientation of the regimes.

In the case of Algeria, the creation of a modernized state sector on the settler farms left 2.8 million hectares to be consolidated into 3,000 units of around 1,000 hectares each. These were to be self-managed by the former workers on the *colon* estates. This meant that around 60% of crop production was vested in state hands. To the extent that self-management, or *autogestion*, as it is termed in Algeria, of state farms can be made co-terminous with state socialism, the colonial withdrawal from Algeria effected a transition from a capitalist to a socialist-dominated agriculture.

This change in production relations on the bulk of Algeria's agricultural land did not change the inequitable distribution of land in areas outside the state sector. In the 1960s, some 20,000 landholders, with holdings of over 50 hectares, owned 25% of the arable land, 147,000 holdings of 10–50 hectares owned 50% of the land and 424,000 holdings of below 10 hectares provided the basis for a minifundist agriculture. On these large units, absentee landownership and share-cropping were to be found together with capitalist enterprises using wage labour.

The Algerian government felt that such differentiations in agriculture were not commensurate with its political beliefs. The government aspired to redistribute access to land in favour of small and landless farmers and to make this class more productive through the medium of co-operatives. By 1972, some one million hectares had been distributed to 60,000 households. In 1972–73 a further round of reforms expropriated all lands from absentee owners and set ceilings of 1–5 hectares for crop land, 12–45 hectares for olive groves and 4–18 hectares for vineyards. The potential area to be distributed covered three million hectares, of which two million were expropriated land. Whilst this reform is much more egalitarian than anything we have identified so far in the Middle East, its beneficiaries still cover only a third of the potential beneficiaries from the ranks of the landless and land-poor. The decision to adhere to the capital-intensive technology inherited from the French in the state farms has thus put limits on the number of potential beneficiaries of agrarian reform. Thus whilst differentiation in the private sector has narrowed, it has not been eliminated, and in this respect the Algerian reform falls short of the radical compass of the Asian reforms.

The replication of the Algerian model in Mozambique and Angola has, of course, encountered major problems. In these countries, for a variety of reasons the new state farms could not achieve performance levels comparable to those realized under Portuguese ownership and agricultural production has fallen. Whilst this is, in part, undoubtedly due to the massive destruction and destabilization inflicted by the South African-sponsored insurgencies, it is evident that, as was the case in Algeria, the state sector has not been able to command the managerial and technical skills previously deployed by the Portuguese settlers on their farms.

5. Non-Egalitarian Agrarian Reforms Without a Social Transition

The great majority of agrarian reforms take place within the prevailing agrarian system. The levels of land redistribution realized within the compass of the reform do not noticeably effect relations of production, although in some cases certain realignments of power within the factions of the dominant class take place. In some cases the reforms bring a system to the borderline of transition or create conditions where market forces may carry through such a transition. Unlike our discussion in the previous chapters, we will minimize discussion of case histories and reflect on the source and the typologies of reform within this category and see how the outcome of such reforms differs from more egalitarian reforms.

As with reforms which effect a social transition, all reforms within the non-transitional category aspire to redistribute some land and to modify tenurial arrangements to provide more security and better terms for tenants. Such redistribution may take place where the feudal or the capitalist mode is dominant. Particularly in Asia, however, where elements of feudalism and capitalism co-exist with a large household sector, agrarian reforms may adjust the social balance within these modes without establishing a clear tendency towards making a particular mode durable. Whatever results from these reforms, it is observable that no noticeable change in the balance of power has preceded the reform or results from it.

The countries listed under the typology of non-transitional reforms are: Latin America: Chile, Ecuador, Colombia, Venezuela, El Salvador, Honduras, Costa Rica and Guatemala; Africa: Zimbabwe and Kenya; Middle East: Tunisia; Asia: India, Pakistan, Sri Lanka, Bangladesh, Thailand, Indonesia and the Philippines.

Redistribution without a social transition in Latin America

Chile

Within this list there is one problematic case where a significant reform was accomplished but did not last long enough to carry through the social transition which was expected. The case in point is Chile where the reforms of the 1960s under the Christian Democratic regime, which were carried forward under the Allende regime, aspired to moderate the domination of a landowning oligarchy. However Chile had its own special features which make direct comparisons with other Latin American countries more difficult. Thus the tenant farmers of Chile, the *inquilinos*, became wage earners on the *haciendas* but retained rights to farm estate plots. The *inquilinos* were reportedly less bound by feudal obligations to the *hacendados* than the *colonatos* of Mexico, Bolivia and Peru (World Bank, 1978). Since the spread of mechanization in Chile commenced earlier and tended to be more widespread than in other Latin American countries, the *hacendados* moved to set up capitalist farms, reduce dependence on the *inquilinos* and hire outside labour for wages. The agrarian reforms in Chile were thus designed to redistribute land held in the large *haciendas* rather than to eradicate feudalism. There was no intention to disturb modern, productive capitalist farms. The idea was to break up large estates into medium-sized holdings and to give more land to the land-poor households.

The proportion of lands distributed by successive reforms in Chile was quite large, 9.5 million hectares, or 47% of total farm land. This makes the reform, measured in terms of land redistributed in 1973, the largest in Latin America after Cuba and Peru. However, the beneficiaries of this reform covered only 13% of all households, which makes the social compass of the reform well below that achieved by the reforms in Mexico, Bolivia, Peru and even Venezuela. This suggested that the main beneficiaries of the reform tended to be the *inquilinos* working on the large estates affected by the reform. Thus 51% of workers of large estates benefited from the reform, compared to 13% of all agricultural families. It was thus not surprising that the reform only marginally reduced the proportion of landless households to total rural households from 57% prior to the reform in 1965 to 53% in 1973, leaving the absolute number of the landless largely undiminished.

The reform effectively eliminated large estates over 80 hectares whose share of land held fell from 55% to 3%. However farms of 20–80 hectares increased in number and their share of land held increased from 22% to 39%. It is thus evident that many large farms reduced themselves to medium-sized capitalist farms after surrendering some of their lands to the reform sector. Thus in the Allende regime the medium-sized farms co-existed with the collective farms set up on the reformed lands. However some 190,000 farms, 66% of the total, with holdings of under five hectares remained untouched by the reform and continued to farm only 1% of all farm land in minifundist holdings. There was thus clearly no social transition effected by the reform beyond the enhancement of the social power of a segment of the *inquilinos* and a moderation in the power of the biggest landowners. The move during the Allende regime to set up associations of poor peasants to seize the larger estates by force brought some 4,000 estates within the reform sector. The military regime which seized power from Allende set out to reverse some of these seizures and to dismantle some of the workers' collectives set up in the reformed sector. Thus the re-adjustment in the balance of power towards the *inquilinos* and away from the capitalist was clearly on the way to being undone by the change in state power after 1973.

Land reform without land redistribution elsewhere

Apart from the reform in Chile, the other reforms within Latin America reflected neither a discernible adjustment in the social balance of power nor any intention to modify the dominant capitalist mode of production. The compass of these reforms remains limited both in terms of the proportion of land involved and the households benefited by it. In Venezuela agrarian reforms affected only 6% of the land. The fact that 35% of households were listed as beneficiaries of the reform merely reflects that a large part of the distributed lands originated in state lands reclaimed at great cost by the government. So, even after the reform, 67% of all land remained under 4,000 large estates of 1,000 hectares and more which account for only 1.4% of all holdings. This class of *hacendados* remained untouched by the reform.

The Venezuelan agrarian reform, which had originated in a series of minor peasant mobilizations under powerful peasant unions, was deflected by offers of state land and prospects for employment in the rapidly expanding non-agricultural sector under the impact of the oil revenues (Warriner, 1969). The fact that only 15% of the population may be classified as rural in 1984 suggests that, unlike most the Latin American countries, the changes in the balance of power in Venezuela have taken place outside the rural areas.

The Venezuelan experience of agrarian reform, which is designed to leave the relations of production intact and the power and properties of the dominant landowners untouched, has been reflected in reforms throughout Latin America. In the case of Ecuador the initiative for an agrarian reform originated from the landowners in the highlands who wanted to convert their class of *hacienda*-tied labour into wage labour free of non-market linkages to the landowners (Murmis, 1982). In this process surplus lands at the periphery of the *haciendas* were surrendered as part of a process of consolidating and capitalizing smaller capitalist agricultural enterprises.

In Colombia, agrarian reforms were largely designed to defuse peasant militancy against the highly inequitable agrarian system which left 3.5% of landowners, farming lands in excess of 1,000 hectares, controlling 66% of the land, whilst one-third of households in northern territories were landless (King, 1977). A wave of land seizures by a mobilized peasantry left large tracts of peripheral land on the latifundia of the large owners under control of squatters. The agrarian reform of 1961 was designed to legalize some of these squats and to generate some surplus land for redistribution. Ceilings under the Colombian reforms were, however, kept vague, rising as high as 2,000 hectares for uncultivated and 100 hectares for intensively cultivated land. By 1970, some three million hectares of surplus land had been identified for settlement by 100,000 new owners, but 91% of the land being distributed was merely formalizing squatters' rights. The 100,000 new owners of land accounted for only 14% of small landholders in Colombia, and 10% of those who need land if we include landless households. Agrarian reform thus appears to have left the agrarian system of Colombia untouched.

Agrarian reform within the capitalist mode of production: Central America

The other group of countries within Latin America to carry through some agrarian reforms without effecting any social transition are to be found in Central America. These include Costa Rica, El Salvador, Guatemala, Honduras and Panama. In these countries, as in the countries of South America, agriculture appears to be highly commercialized with a class of capitalist farmers and corporate holdings controlling the bulk of the land and producing cash crops for the external, largely North American, market. Apart from Panama, which exports 38% of its agricultural output, the other four countries export over 50% of their output, with Costa Rica, exporting 64.3% of its output, at the top of the list (Peek, 1986). Landownership is highly concentrated in Central America, with over 40% of land between 1970–80 held in holdings of over 100 hectares, with the exception of El Salvador where only some 38.70% of the land is held in such large holdings. In contrast, less than 20% of the land is held in holdings of less than 10 hectares, again with El Salvador being the exception, with 27.1% of land in holdings less than 10 hectares. The dominance of the large capitalist plantations is clearly discernible. The importance of foreign, mainly North American, capital is again clearly discernible in these large holdings. The capitalist holdings tend to be highly capital-intensive and employ wage labour drawn both from the attached tenants-at-will leasing in plots of land on the *haciendas* to meet their subsistence needs and the rising proportion of completely landless agricultural workers.

In the wake of the Cuban revolution in 1959, agrarian reforms within Central America became a much promoted issue through the Alliance for Progress (Petras and Laporte, 1971). The idea of using agrarian reforms, designed to give land and security of tenure to the landless, land-poor and tenant farmers of Central America to contain peasant insurgencies, was supported by the liberals of the Kennedy administration who conceived the Alliance. The highly autocratic oligarchies holding state power in most of Central America in the 1960s were, however, not persuaded to attempt to effect a sufficiently radical redistribution of land such as to disturb the power of the *hacendados*.

In Costa Rica, for example, one of the more democratic regimes in Central America, what passed for land reform was really a modest programme of settlement for peasant farmers and titling of uncultivated lands squatted upon by this class. This access to land marginally reduced the very high gini-co-efficient of Costa Rica from 0.8223 in 1973 (Peek, 1986). This left intact the latifundias where 9% of farms with holdings above 100 hectares controlled 68% of the land, and within this category 0.5% of farms held 25% of the land, while 47.8% of farms held 3.8% of the land. It is not surprising that workers from these minifundist holdings, along with those without any land, now swell the class of wage labourers working on capitalist farms. In 1981 it was estimated that 64% of the agricultural labour force was made up of wage workers.

Agrarian reforms in El Salvador were obviously likely to demand more attention than in Costa Rica due to the continuing peasant-based insurgency.

Unlike other Central American countries in this category, El Salvador had in 1971 a more egalitarian pattern of land distribution, which had progressively improved between 1950 and 1971.

Taking US advice and responding to electoral pressure, a phased programme of land reforms in El Salvador had by 1982 appropriated 15% of farm land from 328 large holdings for distribution to 34,728 rural workers, approximately 10–15% of landless households. A second phase, yet to be fully implemented, would have covered an additional 24% of the nation's farmland. A third phase was to have given land rights to some 150,000 tenants working on 4% of agricultural land. However the second and third phases met strong resistance from the large landowners backed by elements within the armed forces, and very little of this has been implemented. If completed, the land reform in El Salvador could have had a redistributive impact of the level attained at least in Bolivia and would have given land rights to *hacienda* tenants who continue in relations of functional dualism as tenants-at-will on the large estates. Such a reform would have kept capitalist relations of production intact, but would have permitted the emergence of a class of minifundist landholders. This class of smallholders could co-exist with the large capitalist holdings, as in Bolivia and Mexico where the large capitalist farms become dependent on supplies of smallholders' labour.

Undoing agrarian reform through external intervention: Guatemala
In contrast to El Salvador, in 1979 in Guatemala 4% of holdings of over 450 hectares held 65% of the land whilst 81% of holdings of 3.5 hectares or less held 10% of the land. At the summit of this pyramid, 0.2% of holdings of more than 450 hectares held 35% of the land whilst at the other end 41% of holdings of 0.7 hectares and below held 10% of the land. This reflects the dominance of US-owned plantations and livestock ranches geared to the US market in the production and exports of the agricultural sector in Guatemala. A high proportion of minifundist farmers obviously earned the larger part of their livelihood working on the large capitalist holdings. One study reports that 70% of harvest workers in large cotton, coffee and sugar farms were part-time labour drawn from the minifundist holdings (Peek, 1986).

Unlike other parts of Central America, no agrarian reform of any consequence has been attempted in recent years in Guatemala. This appears to be the legacy of the ill-fated attempt at agrarian reform in 1953–54 by the Arbenz regime which merely sought to redistribute some of the untilled land held by the large latifundias of the United Fruit Company and other large foreign and local holdings. In 1950, 2.2% of large landowners held four million acres, or 70% of all crop land in Guatemala, but only 25% of this was under cultivation (Schlesinger and Kinzer, 1983). The agrarian reform initiated by Arbenz in 1952 sought to expropriate the uncultivated part of large plantations, defined as holdings of above 223 acres. Indeed holdings between 223 and 670 acres which cultivated up to two-thirds of the acreage in their holdings were also exempted. The expropriated land was to be distributed to landless peasants in holdings not exceeding 42.5 acres. During the 18 months of this programme, 100,000 landless families received 1.5 million acres and 16% of all privately owned fallow land was expropriated (Schlesinger and Kinzer, 1983). Inevitably, this reform hit the holdings of the all-powerful United Fruit Company, the largest landowner in Guatemala, which owned 550,000 acres of land. In 1953 it was estimated that 85% of this land was left uncultivated. The Arbenz reform in 1953–54 moved to expropriate some 386,901 acres, or 77% of the United Fruit Company's holdings, which is somewhat less than the estimate of its surplus holdings (Schlesinger and Kinzer, 1983). Compensation was offered but the terms became an issue of dispute between the Guatemalan government and the company, now reinforced by the full backing of the US government.

This major challenge to the hegemony of US capital over the Guatemalan economy was unacceptable to a United States government then going through a revivalist phase in its foreign policy with John Foster Dulles as Secretary of State. This stand-off between the Arbenz regime and the US government culminated in a CIA-backed military coup, which overthrew the Arbenz regime, undid the agrarian reform and restored most of the expropriated holdings to their former owners (Schlesinger and Kinzer, 1983). The Guatemalan experience of agrarian reform in 1953–54 provides an excellent example of how the domestic balance of power in a small country can be sustained by external forces and any challenge to the prevailing configurations of power can provoke an external intervention to maintain that balance of power.

It is not surprising that Guatemala was one of the few countries in Latin America where distribution of land remained as unequal in 1979 as it had been in 1950 and where no agrarian reforms of any shape were attempted after 1954. The dominance of the agrarian sector by the foreign corporations and the local landed elite, underwritten by a succession of repressive military regimes which held power until the elections of 1987, was thus total. The inequitable agrarian structure and perpetuation of rural poverty was the inevitable consequence of this peculiar balance of power in Guatemala.

Honduras
Honduras was yet another Central American country heavily dependent on export of cash crops with its agrarian structure dominated by foreign-owned plantations and a local landed elite operating large *haciendas* within an essentially capitalist mode of production. In 1974, 4% of farms of 100 hectares or more operated 55% of the farm area whilst 64% of farms of five hectares and less operated 9% of all farm land. A further 150,000 households, 43% of the rural total, were landless (Peek, 1986). This meant that some 80% of households were landless or land-poor and had to sell their labour mainly to the *haciendas* to ensure their survival.

Whilst there was some peasant mobilization in Honduras, which alerted the military junta that seized power in 1972 to take cognisance of the conditions of the rural poor, nothing occurred to challenge the hegemony of the large foreign and local landowning elite which dominated the Honduran state.

The *soi-disant* reforms of 1972 initiated by the military regime, as in Costa Rica, Venezuela and Colombia, in fact consisted of assigning state lands to landless households. Such a reform did not need to disturb the holdings or the power base of the landowning elite, the prevailing relations of production or the system of functional dualism whereby the minifundist farmers sold their labour to capitalist *hacendados*.

The distribution of state lands was, however, not insignificant and was comparable in its dimensions to the Venezuelan rather than the Costa Rican distribution of state lands. The amount of land distributed under the 1972 reform between 1972 and 1981 came to 251,372 hectares, or 4% of all privately owned land (Peek, 1986). This went to 49,855 households, or nearly one-third of landless households, and increased the number of holdings below five hectares by 86%, from 57% of all farms in 1952 to 64%. The reform was significant in that at the margin it arrested the growth of landlessness, but did so by adding to the numbers of minifundist farmers.

This access to land thus yielded no noticeable redistribution of land held by the upper echelons of the agrarian hierarchy of Honduras, although there was some redistribution between holdings of above 500 hectares and those between 100 and 500 hectares. In the best traditions of landowning elites around the world seeking to protect themselves against prospective land reform, many of the units of more than 500 hectares were reparcelled so that, whilst land in holdings above 500 hectares declined from 28% of all holdings in 1952 and 22% in 1974, land in holdings of 100–500 hectares increased from 18% to 22% and the aggregate of lands held in holdings of above 100 hectares remained constant at around 1.16 million hectares (Peek, 1986).

Notwithstanding the fact that there was some attempt to promote joint production through co-operatives on the reclaimed lands and the prevalence of *ejido* tenure amongst the small farmers, as in Mexico, improved access to the land for the landless disturbed the functional dualism imposed on the minifundist landholdings. The supply of surplus labour from the minifundist holdings, along with the residual of 100,000 landless households left untouched by the 1972 reforms, ensured a ready supply of cheap labour to sustain the profitability of the capitalist mode of production on the large *haciendas*.

Panama

Panama's agrarian structure was not dissimilar to that of other Central American countries, with heavy dependence on export crops, the dominance of capitalist farms and a highly inegalitarian land ownership structure. In 1970, 4% of farms with holdings above 100 hectares held 46% of the land, whilst 60% of holdings of below 10 hectares accounted for 8% of the land, and 108 holdings of more than 1,000 hectares with an average farm size of 3,158 hectares held 16% of the land.

Agrarian reform in Panama, as in all of Central America except Sandinista Nicaragua and Guatemala in 1954, was carried out from above without any change in the domestic balance of power. Unlike the Costa Rican and Honduran reforms, however, the reforms in Panama had incorporated a modest element of land redistribution; 220 farms with total holdings of 330,000 hectares were acquired by the government. This covered 7% of all holdings above 100 hectares in 1970 and 15.7% of all agricultural land. It was distributed to 17,703 landless and land-poor households, 12% of all rural landowning households or 31% of all landless holdings.*

Not all the beneficiaries of the Panamanian reform were landless, and included some middle peasants with the capacity to run a small commercial farm. The reforms thus left production relations undisturbed and rural society dominated by a small capitalist class.

The Central American experience of agrarian reform thus suggests that, as in the rest of Latin America, with the exceptions of Cuba and, to a certain extent, Nicaragua, much of the agrarian reform was essentially marginal in nature. It was enacted in societies where capitalist agriculture, catering for an export market and with a heavy external presence, was the dominant mode of production. The reforms were thus designed to provide some redress to the growing class of landless households by giving them access to either state lands or untilled lands from the large commercial *haciendas*. No attempt was made either to realize a more equitable distribution of land or to disturb the relations of production. No social transition thus contributed to the reform or resulted from it. The one case where some change in the domestic balance of power permitted an agrarian reform, in Guatemala in 1954, was undone through a counter-revolution underwritten by external power. In such societies marked by heavy external penetration of the economy, a change in the domestic balance of power may not be enough and may well face an external challenge. Where this challenge comes from a superpower, agrarian reform in a particular country becomes a factor in the regional balance of power and cannot be seen as an issue to be resolved within the confines of domestic political struggles.

Social systems in transition: agrarian reform in South Asia

Outside Latin America the other significant set of agrarian reforms within the prevailing relations of production are to be found in Asia. Here, however, the South Asian experience has certain specific features which make it arguable whether relations of production have indeed remained undisturbed. It is still being debated whether agrarian reforms have effectively eradicated feudalism and a form of capitalism has now emerged as the dominant mode of production in agriculture (Khan, 1985). It would thus be appropriate to characterize the South Asian agrarian system as being in transition, but it is arguable that this transitional state owes less to agrarian reform than to the impact of technological change.

* This figure is indirectly derived from Peek, 1986 which gives no figure for landless households. It assumes a household size of five in Panama. This gives a rural landowning population in 1970 of (92,000 x 5) 460,000. If total rural population is 748,000 then the landless population must be 288,000 (748,000 – 460,000) and landless households 57,600 (288,000 ÷ 5).

The four South Asian countries, India, Pakistan, Bangladesh and Sri Lanka, have all initiated a variety of agrarian reforms. It is arguable that although a particular fraction of the feudal classes has effectively been eliminated as a social force in India, Bangladesh and Sri Lanka, aspects of feudalism, in the form of the persistence of share-cropping and the survival of non-market relations between landlord and tenant, remain a dominant feature of the social scene in these countries.

In the case of India, the decolonization process noticeably affected the dominant position of the upper echelons of feudal classes at the level of the rajahs, nawabs and zamindars. This class had either had its power reinforced by the colonial power, or had indeed been specifically vested by the colonial power with rent-receiving interests in the land, so as to serve as bulwarks for the colonial strategy of indirect rule. Thus one of the first by-products of the British withdrawal from India was the spate of land reform legislation which sought to reduce the power of the feudal lords exercised through their monopoly over land (Herring, 1985).

Old landlords for new: the case of Bangladesh

In what is now Bangladesh, as in many parts of India, the proprietory rights of superior rent-receiving interests vested in a class of landlords by the British were withdrawn both through the imposition of land ceilings and resumption of rent-receiving interests by the state (Jannuzi and Peach, 1982). In Bangladesh the task was facilitated by the fact that the landlord class was largely Hindu whilst the tenants and voters were Muslims. The legislators in the East Bengal provincial assembly of the newly independent state of Pakistan had few links with the class of erstwhile landowners who had in most cases opted to become citizens of India rather than Pakistan.

In Bangladesh, as in those Indian states where feudal influences were noticeable, the diminished power, prestige and authority associated with the withdrawal of imperial patronage gave strength to the new social forces associated with the ruling Congress Party in India or the Muslim League in East Pakistan to legislate reforms directly cutting at the power base of the feudal elites.

Neither in Bangladesh or India, however, did land reforms lead to any sizeable control over land by the state, either for redistribution or operation by the state. In Bangladesh, an intermediary class of tenure holders became the principal beneficiary of the reform and new patterns of land concentration and monopoly of political power came to substitute the paramountcy of the feudal classes. Landlessness and rural povery have persisted in Bangladesh and landownership remains no less concentrated even after the exit of the feudal landlords as a dominant class. Thus in 1978 in Bangladesh 3% of housholds controlled 26% of the agricultural land and an estimated 78% of rural households could be classified as landless or almost landless (Jannuzi and Peach, 1982). Since the 1950 reforms in Bangladesh, efforts at further land distribution have been negligible. Indeed the ceiling of the 1950 reform set at 33 acres was revised upwards to 100 acres in the 1960s. This was lowered in 1972, after independence from Pakistan, to 33 acres, but land appropriated and redistributed under the 1972 reform remains negligible (Siddiqui, 1980).

The social transformations which have eroded the power of the feudal classes in post-colonial South Asia had no corresponding manifestation elsewhere, except perhaps in the specific case of both parts of Korea and Taiwan, where the colonial power was also the dominant landlord.

The closest parallel to the assault on feudalism in South Asia relates to the overthrow of the Middle Eastern monarchies associated with British paramountcy in the country and with a class of emirs and pashas who constituted the basis of Middle Eastern feudalism. The loss of rights to ground rent did not mean that the old zamindar disappeared as a socio-political factor in the countryside of South Asia. In the case of Bangladesh, we have seen this was made inevitable because of the peculiar communal character of the nation-state of Pakistan, although the subordinate tenure holders who took over the land assumed tenancy rights vacated by the Hindu zamindars and established new relations of dependency over the share-croppers.

In parts of India, particularly in such states as Bihar, Uttar Pradesh, Andhra Pradesh and Rajasthan, the old landlords managed to retain through various measures of clandestine re-appropriation their title to sizeable holdings of land and with it much of the feudal authority in the village (Haque and Sirohi, 1986).

In other cases in India, however, this class retreated to the towns and as in Bangladesh surrendered rural power to the small landlord and rich farmers. In a democratic polity this new class become the political support-base for the urban-based political leaders. They could thus greatly enhance their social authority by acting as intermediaries between poor peasants and the state, and in the process they become the strongest bulwarks against further agrarian reforms designed to modify the balance of power in the countryside. Since partition this class has remained a powerful influence in the councils of the principal political parties in India, East Pakistan and now Bangladesh.

Share-cropping: its persistence in the post-reform phase

Significantly enough, the initial elimination of the superior landlord did not in most cases lead to the emergence of a class of peasant capitalists managing the land and hiring in labour. This class emerged as a by-product of the green revolution rather than from the post-independence agrarian reforms of the sub-continent. In the wake of these initial reforms, the class of subordinate tenure-holders who acquired title to land largely chose to let their land be tilled by share-cropping tenant farmers who were either without land or needed to rent additional land to augment their own holdings in order to ensure their subsistence. Thus unlike the Latin American model, the new landowners in the post-reform phase in South Asia remained alienated from the land. This class, however, unlike the zamindars of the British period, was not an absentee landlord but maintained his presence in the countryside and was a dominant social and political force there. This class reinforced its control over land with interventions in the water, credit, inputs and even the commodity market.

The green revolution significantly enhanced the economic power of this class as the new technology greatly increased the importance of access to credit and inputs offered at subsidized rates by institutional sources. The rich farmers were the appropriate brokers with the state to mediate the flow of these modernizing resources to the cultivating classes.

The prospects of enhanced returns from the land made it inevitable that the returns from ground rent and acting as intermediaries could now be compounded by increasing returns from the direct management of the land. Rich farmers' superior access to inputs and capital therefore drove them along the path from petty landlordism to capitalist farming.

It is noticeable that in South Asia the green revolution has not altogether eliminated the phenomenon of share-cropping, and in some cases may have contributed to its growth. Thus in Bangladesh between 1960 and 1977 the proportion of households share-cropping in some land increased from 39% to 41.6%, whilst the proportion of land share-cropped in remained unchanged in the region of 45% (Wahab and Sen, 1986). The bulk of this share-cropping was carried on not by a class of pure tenants, who indeed remain proportionately insignificant, but by minifundist holdings renting in land to enhance their capability for subsistence.

In Pakistan, whilst there was a discernible decline in holdings leasing in land, from 58% in 1972 to 45% in 1980, and of land leased in from 60% to 48%, land under tenancy still remained high by Third World standards. Indeed in 1980, some 26% of all farms and 22% of all land was still under pure tenancy. Only in India was there a discernible decline in share-cropping, at least according to official estimates but, as we will see later, these figures may not reflect the exact position.

To equate share-cropping with feudalism is, of course, hardly justified. As we have indicated earlier, in South Asia a part of the land is leased out on the basis of crop shares by smallholders who have migrated to the city or even entered the rural labour market because of the inability of their land to ensure subsistence, and these members of the rural population can hardly be classified as feudal lords. Conversely it is quite normal for landowners to lease out some land, work other parts with hired labour and to switch the modes from season to season on different plots of land. It is also not unusual for a big farmer to supervise production on share-cropped land where he may be supplying the inputs. The practise of breaking up tasks in the crop cycle is common in Indonesia and the Philippines, where labour is hired in during the harvest for a 20% share of the crop. In the Philippines this custom is known as *hunos*. This practice is not unknown in South Asia, but the tradition there is to pay harvest workers a daily wage and/or some meals.

The equation of share-cropping with feudalism is thus hazardous and can only be justified if tracts of land are rented out for long periods of time to customary tenants with whom the landowners establish a stable patron–client relationship. Here ties on the land are reinforced by customary non-market ties. The available evidence from South Asia suggests that this relationship is, with some exceptions, being eroded by the growth of market relations between even the share-cropper and the landlord. The landowner now makes market-determined decisions based on available cropping, technological and investment options, and notions of risk aversion. Share-cropping of high-yield varieties cropped land is often a market decision designed to transfer the investment cost and risk of crop failure to the tenant. As land becomes scarce, rental values are kept stable but the scarcity premium on access to land may be discounted against non-market services. Thus even such non-market services have acquired an opportunity cost and now have to be purchased on the market against access to scarce land rented at below its opportunity cost and/or wages at above their scarcity value.

The role of agrarian reform in effecting the transition from feudalism to capitalism has thus only arisen in the context of a technological breakthrough which has converted scarce land into a commodity with high opportunity cost. Redistributive land reform, by reducing the holdings at the disposal of the erstwhile landowner, has in many cases, with access to new technology, compelled him to concentrate his capital on a lower concentration of land, thus effectively raising the capital—land ratio. The emergence of the capitalist farmer using deep-tube wells, modern machinery and hired labour and managing the land himself or through hired managers, in the Latin American tradition, has emerged in some parts of India, for example where holdings illegitimately retained have provided the economies of scale needed to effect a transition to capitalism.

Transition to capitalism within a feudal mode: Pakistan

This tendency for feudal lords to evolve into capitalist farmers was much more likely in Pakistan, where the successive land reforms permitted high retention limits. The agrarian reforms of 1959 under the martial law regime of Ayub Khan set ceilings of 600 acres on irrigated land and 1,000 acres for rain-fed land, with further generous exclusions under various heads. It was not unusual for families, using exemptions under the law and clandestine redistributions, to retain units of 2,000 to 3,000 acres (Khan, 1981). It was thus not surprising that only 1.6% of agricultural land in Pakistan was covered by the reform. The recovered land covered only 25% of lands owned by 6,061 landowners with holdings of over 500 acres. Only 50% of this resumed land was sold to tenants, the remainder being largely identified as uncultivable. It is estimated that 40% of land distributed under the reform was sold to only 67,000 landless and land-poor households, 2% of the country's peasants. The remainder was auctioned off, and much of it was bought by rich farmers (Khan, 1981).

The 1959 reform in Pakistan was thus minimal in its redistributive impact and in eroding the power of the landlords as a class. However, the reform coincided with the advent of the green revolution and it has been argued that the simultaneous advent of the new technology and the 1959 agrarian reform created conditions for the landlords as a class to switch over to taking greater managerial interest over some of their retained land, even those parts which were still share-cropped out (Khan, 1981).

The tendency was further accentuated by the 1972 land reforms enacted, again under martial law but by a populist elected government led by Bhutto, himself a powerful landlord in Sind. The Bhutto regime reduced the ceiling of land retained by the former owner to 150 acres of irrigated land and 300 acres for rain-fed land, but again permitted various exemption clauses designed to promote capitalist farming using capital-intensive techniques. One estimate reckons that these exemptions in effect raised the ceiling for irrigated land up to 932/1,120 acres (Khan, 1981). It was thus not surprising that this legislation did not net more than 590,000 acres of cultivable land which could be assigned to only 73,000 households, or 1% of all landless and land-poor agricultural households (Khan, 1981).

A third reform, enacted by the Bhutto regime in 1977, sought to reduce the ceiling to 100 acres for irrigated and 200 acres for unirrigated land. This reform was overtaken by the overthrow of the Bhutto regime in 1977 by yet another military coup. It is not clear if this latest reform would have been any more effective in redistributing land than the 1959 or 1972 reforms. It is, however, likely that after the 1972 reforms the threat of new reforms had encouraged divestiture of land within the family and to other clients of the landlord so that retained holdings were enough to enable the landlords to sustain a viable capitalist holding. The transition to capitalist farming was thus accelerated after 1972 when cultivation of the retained holdings became even more capital-intensive.

Unlike both India and Bangladesh, the original class of zamindars or superior rent-receiving interests created by the British in Pakistan was not supplanted by the land reforms of 1961 or 1972. The traditional landlords, particularly in the Punjab and Sind, remained socially and politically powerful and were a dominant element in the Pakistan legislature of 1962 and even 1970. However in 1970, at least in the Punjab, some of the biggest landowners were defeated by smaller landowners supporting Bhutto's People's Party, but in Sind even the People's Party drew on the support of the dominant feudal families. During the 1977 election Bhutto gave party tickets to many of the most powerful zamindar families of the Punjab to contest the elections, whilst the representation from Sind continued to be dominated by the large zamindars. In elections held under martial law in 1986, as well as the parliamentary elections of 1989 and 1990, a large part of the national legislature was drawn from Pakistan's leading zamindar families. Thus after two land reforms over some 30 years the landlord class which dominated the socio-political life of the Punjab and Sind in the pre-1959 land reform period is still politically powerful. Whether in fact these reforms, interacting with the green revolution, have effected a transition in the relations of production from feudalism to capitalism depends on a characterization of these concepts in the specific conditions of Pakistan. The case for the transition to capitalism in Pakistan has been most persuasively argued by Mahmud Hasan Khan who cites supporting evidence to indicate that:

these changes in the renting or leasing of land between various sizes of farms indicate that poor peasants are increasingly renting out their lands to rich peasants. Secondly, landlords are renting out less land to share-croppers.

Thirdly, capitalist farms are increasing in the Punjab and Sind at the expense of poor and even middle-class peasants in the former and against landlords and their share-croppers in the latter province (Khan, 1985).

Khan and some Indian scholars (Patnaik) equate capitalism with the replacement of share-cropping by use of wage labour and trace this transition in terms of the rise of a class of farmers operating holdings of between 25 and 150 acres, largely renting in rather than renting out land (Khan, 1985). He does not, however, specify the social characteristics of his class stereotype so that we do not know how many of the erstwhile landowners transformed themselves into capitalist farmers so that the capitalist farmer and feudal lord co-exist in the same family as do capitalist relations of production and the system of share-cropping on the same ownership holdings. It would appear that the old style zamindar share-cropping his land and living the luxurious life of an absentee landlord is at least in Pakistan a thing of the past. The contemporary landowner, not much less powerful today than he was prior to the original reforms of 1959, operates a capitalist enterprise within his estate, with professional managers, using mechanized irrigation and heavy tractors and has invested in sugar and textile mills. He is thus far removed from the erstwhile zamindars of British India and much closer to the modern capitalist *hacendados* of Latin America.

Elimination of capitalist relations of production? Sri Lanka

The experience in Sri Lanka was slightly different from that of the rest of the sub-continent. Control over land was exercised by a class of absentee landowners owning medium-sized holdings of paddy land which were share-cropped. This class was, however, not a powerful force in the rural areas where power vested with a rural petty bourgeoisie, with some interest in land and other sources of income from jobs in the service sector, as school teachers, indigenous physicians, astrologers and small traders (Gunasinghe, 1982). The other sources of income from jobs in the service sector, such as school teachers, which were capitalist enclaves in the Sri Lankan countryside controlled by foreign capital (in tea) and an indigenous capitalist class.

The agrarian reforms carried out between 1972 and 1975 by the Bandranaike administration originated as a response to the armed uprising provoked by a radical political party drawing its support from the educated youth of rural petty-bourgeois origin (Gunasinghe, 1982; Herring, 1985). The initial reform in 1972 appropriated 563,411 acres of paddy land from the landowners. The reform was very generous and set ceilings which could effectively exclude the absentee owners of paddy lands. The individual holdings of land of the Sinhalese landlords appropriated under the reform amounted to only 18,407 acres, or 4.7%, of paddy lands. In contrast, the 1972 reform hit at lands engaged in cultivation of cash crops, and the land affected included 41.5% of tea, rubber and coconut plantations and 31.9% of uncultivated land.

The second round of the reforms in 1975 completed the task of eradicating the capitalist holdings in the plantation sector of Sri Lanka. A further 417,975 acres of plantation lands, including 56.8% of all tea plantation land and 22.5% of land under rubber plantations, were acquired. These included 221,356 acres held in 180 Sterling estates and 196,601 acres held in 215 national estates. The reform thus not only hit the indigenous capitalist class but effectively removed the hold of foreign capital on the plantation sector. Unlike a number of the non-egalitarian reforms reviewed so far, the Sri Lankan reform is thus unique in eliminating capitalism as a relation of production in the countryside whilst leaving intact elements of feudalism in the form of absentee ownership and share-cropping, with production in the hands of small owners and tenant farmers operating within a subsistence agriculture.

The appropriated plantation lands in Sri Lanka were incorporated into the state sector to be farmed as state enterprises or production co-operatives rather than redistributed as minifundist holdings. In this respect the Sri Lankan reforms parallel those in Peru, Chile and Algeria where the substitution of a capitalist by non-capitalist or state sector was the favoured option. The enlarged state sector in Sri Lanka was then used to provide employment opportunities for the educated rural youth who had been at the vanguard of the 1971 insurgency. This attempt to use the agrarian reform to defuse tensions in the countryside has contributed to the erosion of the surplus generated by these commercial enterprises now reconstituted as part of the state sector in agriculture.

The relevant change in the balance of power, if any, in Sri Lanka was thus effected at the national level where a regime sensitive to the concerns of the lower middle class attacked plantation interests in the agricultural sector with a view to damping down the militancy of that rural petty bourgeoisie. It is to be seen whether those reforms will promote equality in rural Sri Lanka since they do not directly help the poor peasant or tenant farmer. Nor is it clear how far the reforms will maintain productive forces and the level of surplus generated from the capitalist plantations.

India: a transition to capitalist agriculture?

Of all the South Asian countries, India appears to have made the most rapid advance in the transition to capitalist relations of production in the wake of agrarian reform and technological change. This trend in the emergence of capitalist relations of production in India is manifest in the fact that, except in the tribal areas of the north-east of the country, the incidence of tenancy cultivation has declined sharply. At the time of independence, 35.7% of the cultivated area of India was under tenancy. According to the 1976–77 Agricultural Census of India, only 2.2% of the cropped land was under tenancy, and only in the hill states of Manipur, Tripura and Sikkim did the area under tenancy exceed 10%. Only in two states, West Bengal (7.1%) and the hill state of Himachal Pradesh (6.7%) does it now exceed 5% (Haque and Sirohi, 1986). The census figures are, however, contradicted by some micro-studies which suggest higher rates of tenancy: 38% in Bihar, 20% in one district of the Punjab and 32% in one district of Burdwan (Haque and Sirohi, 1986). This suggests that census estimates of a reduction in tenancy may be exaggerated and could possibly conceal the co-existence of tenancy and self-cultivation in the same holdings with the occupant declaring such holdings to be owned. This would be consistent with our hypothesis that the advent of the green revolution has indeed encouraged landowners in India to transfer part of their land, whether by area or cropping season, to share-croppers who will bear the risk of the investment. In areas such as Bihar (30.8%), the Punjab (49.7%) and West Bengal (83.9%), where tenancy is seen as being more pervasive than is suggested in the census, it is share-cropping which is the most favoured mode of tenancy in comparison to fixed rent or fixed produce modes (Haque and Sirohi, 1986).

This hypothesis needs to be tested through more detailed studies. However the tendency to mix tenancy with owner-cultivation implies a notion of profit maximization associated with capitalist relations of production so that the mere presence of tenancy need not be equated with the archaic form of production associated with absentee owners leasing out their lands to a subaltern class of impoverished share-croppers. Indeed the evidence in India, as in Pakistan, suggests that it is the minifundist as much as the middle and large farmer associated with a capitalist mode of production who may be leasing in land. Thus at the all-India level, nearly 40% of the leased in land was accounted for by holdings of 4–10 hectares (middle farmers) and above 10 hectares (large farmers). Indeed, the share of this class rose from 40% in 1970–71 to 43.7% in 1976–77, and within this the share of leased in land retained by holdings of over 10 hectares averaged from 15.9% to 18.7%. By 1976–77, in some states such as Andhra Pradesh (61.8%), Haryana (51.9%), Madhya Pradesh (71.4%) and the Punjab (49.1% in 1970–71), the bulk of the leasing in has been done by the medium and large farmers. To the extent that the green revolution has made a significant impact in these states, the emergence of the capitalist farmer with an expanded, more capital-intensive and self-managed enterprise using hired labour is a discernible trend in India, associated less with agrarian reform than with the changing profitability of agriculture associated with the new technology.

That this tendency towards capitalist farming should coincide with the growth of minifundist holdings and landless rural households is not surprising. The number of households operating less than one hectare increased from 38.4% of all holdings in 1950–51 to 54.6% in 1976–77, and the area under these holdings also increased from 6% to 10.7% (Haque and Sirohi, 1986). Minifundist households were obviously having to sell their labour to the larger capitalist holdings to maintain subsistence. A version of functional dualism associated with Latin America was thus not entirely absent from South Asia, and this class of minifundists was having to compete in the labour market with landless households with only their labour to sell. This class increased from 27.5 million in 1951 to 85.4 million in 1981 (Haque and Sirohi, 1986). There was, however, a marginal decline from 26.9% in 1971 to 25.2% in 1981 in the proportion of agricultural labourers in relation to total households. But this suggests that land-poor (those with below one hectare) and landless households in the rural areas account for around 80% of rural households who have to sell their labour to guarantee their subsistence. India has, therefore, witnessed the emergence of capitalist relations of production in which a small class of capitalist farmers rent in land and hire in the labour of a growing rural proletariat. This appears to be the end-product of a succession of agrarian reforms in India, which by 1985 had distributed 1.8 million hectares, 3.5% of all operational holdings in the country in 1981 (Raju, 1986). This figure does not include an estimated 55 million agricultural labourers, so if we assume the total agricultural labour force in India to be 149 million in 1981, then the proportion of land reform beneficiaries comes to 2% of the total and 5.8% of the class of agricultural labourers. This conceals considerable regional differentiation in the incidence of the reform, but stil shows how limited its impact has been on India's rural population.

The limited impact of the agrarian reforms in India reflects the new configurations in the social balance of power in the country once the feudal rent-receiving interests created by the British raj were eliminated. The new, more numerous, class of middle and large farmers is well entrenched in the hierarchy of power in the local community and effectively constitutes the bridge between the tillers of the soil, be they minifundist farmers, share-croppers or agricultural labourers, and the machinery of state.

Only in one state, Kerala, which has had long periods of Communist or left-wing rule, has this new balance of power been effectively breached and the system of tenancy abolished in the process. In Kerala, after a succession of agrarian reforms aimed at eliminating share tenancy as a relation of production, 36.5% of the net sown area had been distributed to 43% of all agricultural households in the state (Herring, 1985). Not all of this necessarily went to poor peasants, and one estimate reckons that 38.7% of this land went to rich peasants who leased in land, and that poor and middle peasants, defined as households with less than five acres, received 36.2% of the land. The smallest peasant holding of less than one acre, accounting for 16.6% of households, held only 0.9% of the reformed land. The capitalist revolution appears to have been frustrated in Kerala by the intervention of agrarian reform, and in its place a class of minifundist peasant proprietors now lives in uneasy co-existence with a rising number of landless agricultural households and a small class of rich farmers with holdings above 10 acres who number 4,000 households which, in 1976–77, was 0.1% of all farm households, who control only 4% of the farm area.

The lesson from India appears to be that the change in the balance of power in the countryside and the state could not really effect a noticeable redistribution in access to land so that the incidence of landlessness and poverty remained high. The green revolution rather than agrarian reform has effected a transition from a feudal to a capitalist mode of production in most parts of India. As in Pakistan, elements of feudalism co-exist with capitalism, but with an increasing tendency for an imperfect market to influence the evolution in the relations of production so that even the share-cropping landlord is now making his decisions in the market place rather than according to inherited customs and social conditioning.

South Asia: a system in transition

The South Asian agrarian reforms have certain features in common with the Latin American and Middle Eastern reforms. With perhaps the exception of Sri Lanka, the reforms in South Asia redistributed much smaller areas of land to a much narrower segment of the rural population, though there are exceptions to this pattern, as in the case of Kerala (Herring, 1985). The Sri Lankan reform must be deemed more radical in terms of its assault on the capitalist sector in agriculture, which has no parallel in the other three countries. The social transition which we have identified in the Middle East, Mexico, Bolivia and possibly Peru has its equivalent possibly in Sri Lanka. This is not to say that, as in Latin America, a change in production relations in Pakistan and in India towards capitalist agriculture has not taken place. But this co-exists with share-cropping throughout South Asia, including Sri Lanka, to an extent without parallel in either Latin America or those parts of the Middle East which have had reforms. This reflects the tenacity of the peasant mode of production where smallholders survive by renting in some land and selling their labour to the new capitalist farmers. This phenomenon may be peculiar to Monsoon Asia where land–labour ratios are unusually low compared to other regions, and appears to have precluded the emergence of capitalist agriculture on as widespread a scale as in the other regions.

Whilst the emergence of capitalism as the dominant mode of production is nowhere near as apparent in South Asia as it is in Latin America, at least in India and Pakistan the emergence, as the dominant social force, of a class of large farmers producing for the market is clearly discernible. This class may be derived from a renovated landlord class, as in Pakistan and parts of India, or from the subordinate tenure-holders empowered by agrarian reforms in post-independence India, or indeed a class of middle/rich peasants or bullock capitalists in India, Pakistan and even Bangladesh. This class is clearly differentiated from the mass of the peasantry by its willingness to adapt capital-intensive technology, make decisions based on market forces, hire in labour and even land and use share-cropping as a market-induced decision. This class may have some way to go before it resembles the *hacendados* of Brazil, Mexico and Venezuela with latifundias of 1,000 hectares or more, but at least some of the new capitalist landlords of Pakistan and India, with the tractors, tube-wells and diversified investments in industry, now share membership of the same social family.

South-East Asia: the transition to peasant capitalism

The agrarian reforms enacted in Thailand, Indonesia and the Philippines were effected without disturbing the relations of production and without any change in the domestic balance of power. They were essentially top-down reforms, though in all three cases the reforms represented, in varying degrees, responses to peasant mobilizations of varying intensity.

In the case of Indonesia, access to land was never very inequitable: 92% of households in Java owned land less than one hectare, but three million peasants were landless. Agrarian reform under the Soekarno regime was, however, sensitive to pressures from a peasant movement spearheaded by the largest Communist party outside the socialist world (Huizer, 1972). The agrarian reform of 1960 sought to give land to the tiller and to limit the ceiling on holdings to 5–15 hectares. Scope for exemptions raised the ceilings. Resistance by religious organizations and tardiness in implementation by the bureaucracy stimulated direct action by peasant organizations under the leadership of the Communist Party to expropriate land for redistribution within the ambit of the land reform laws. By 1964, 355,577 hectares had been acquired from 27,388 owners and 83% of this was distributed to 592,958 families, who accounted for 19.6% of landless families. Some 150,000 acres of this land was, however, reported to have been reclaimed by its original owners after the military coup of 1965 and the subsequent massacre of Communist cadres. A second stage of this reform was expected to increase the lands appropriated under the reform to 938,901 hectares. This phase was delayed, and when resumed in 1968 distributed 388,198 hectares, bringing the total of land distributed under the 1960 reform to 682,698 hectares of cultivable land. This went to a total of 866,983 households, or an estimated 29% of landless households.

It should, however, be noted that of this distributed land, two-thirds was state land so that land appropriated from the landlords or rich peasants was hardly likely to make a dent in the resources or power of the dominant classes in the Indonesian countryside. The fact that only 61% of the land appropriated from landowners was distributed is a measure of the power retained by this class.

Given the capitalist orientation of the Indonesian state after 1965, agrarian reforms were not actively encouraged. The annihilation of the Indonesian Communist Party and the absence of representative institutions meant that there was no scope for peasant mobilization to press for agrarian reform. The fact that a class of middle/rich peasants was the dominant social force in the rural areas meant that further redistributive reforms were only feasible through a more pervasive restructuring in the rural balance of power in favour of the landless and land-poor classes in rural Indonesia.

The emphasis after 1970 on programmes for providing more diffused access to land switched to ambitious capital-intensive programmes of resettlement of landless/land-poor peasants from Java to reclaimed lands in the less populated outlying islands of the Indonesian archipelago. Contemporary evidence suggests that the capital costs of such settlement schemes and social resistance to them has resulted in only a modest reduction in large-scale landlessness in the Javanese countryside. It was estimated that in 1983, out of 25.1 million agricultural households, 27% were landless and 38% had holdings of less than 0.5 hectare (Ahmed, 1987). Indonesian agriculture thus continues to be characterized by considerable differentiation between a class of rich farmers leasing out surplus land and/or hiring labour and a large group of landless/land-poor households which depends on wage labour to survive. It should however be kept in mind that whatever inequalities persist in the

Indonesian rural areas, poorer peasants are better off than their South Asian counterparts due to their higher productivity derived from the more pervasive impact of new high-yield varieties technology in the Indonesian countryside.

As in Indonesia, agrarian reform in Thailand was limited in its coverage. In Thailand access to land was much less severely constrained than in Indonesia or indeed South Asia. Landlessness in Thailand, at around 13%, is one of the lowest in Monsoon Asia. The ownership was also less skewed and the gini-coefficient for land distribution declined from 0.47 in 1962 to 0.43 in 1974, which again was one of the lowest in the developing world (Turton, 1982).

The recent trend in Thailand, common to much of Monsoon Asia, is for a new class of capitalist farmers to invest in land; this class may be drawn from the urban bourgeoisie, both foreign and Thai, corporate investors in plantation crops such as pineapple, and some reconstituted elements of the erstwhile landed elite seeking to reclaim leased out land for capitalist farming. The emergence of this class co-exists with a powerful class of absentee landowners who lease out their lands on a crop-sharing basis. One study estimates that in 1975 some 20% of paddy land, made up of one million acres of land, was owned by absentee landowners. Another estimate shows that in four provinces around Bangkok, 119 absentee landlords, with holdings of 400 acres and above, hold around 150,000 acres of land. Thus in 1976 it was reckoned that 21% of agricultural households rented the land they farmed.

The pressure for agrarian reform in Thailand was never strong. Peasant mobilization, whilst not insignificant, was never at a level to threaten the balance of power in a polity where absentee landlords and capitalists were dominant in both the countryside and the state itself. A moderate land reform enacted in 1954, which sought to impose a ceiling of eight hectares per person, was abolished in 1959 when scope for commercial agriculture was becoming more evident.

A further reform in 1977 reflected the importance of commercial agriculture and the attempt to effect a social transition from a class of absentee landlords to capitalist agriculture. A new ceiling of 20 acres was set to hit at absentee landlords, but holdings of up to 4,000 acres were permitted if they involved large investments. This was designed to promote corporate farming using capital-intensive techniques. A further provision permitted retentions up to 400 acres provided this was not leased out but worked directly by the owner.

A reform with such generous clauses to promote large-scale capitalist farming was hardly likely to be significant in its coverage. Between 1976 and 1979 some 300,000 hectares of tenanted land had been reclaimed, but of this only 1,000 were acquired for vesting ownership on the tenants. Of 650,000 hectares of state lands earmarked for distribution by 1979, only 1,233 farmers had received land.

The reforms thus neither effectively distributed land to the landless nor put sufficient pressure on absentee owners to effect a transition from share tenancy to capitalist agriculture. The transition which actually took place did so in response to market forces and opportunities provided by new technology. The old absentee landowning elite and the new market-oriented corporate farmers today co-exist with the urban bourgeoisie of traders, industrialists, the army and state bureaucracy. In the rural areas, however, power appears to be vested in a new rural middle class in transition between share-cropping and self-cultivation. This class has evolved as the intermediary between the state and the peasantry, and the scope for agrarian reform which could challenge its hegemony would require a level of mobilization extending in scope and intensity well beyond the mobilizations thus far accomplished by such organizations as the Peasant Federation of Thailand and the insurgencies in the border regions of the country. The new rural middle class is well entrenched in the local power structures.

The Philippines: social transitions and persistent differentiation

The agrarian reform carried out in the Philippines in 1972 under the martial law proclaimed by President Marcos has been described as one of the most far-reaching outside the Communist world (Meliczek, 1980). The reform originated in the need to counteract the protracted Hukabalahop insurgency on the island of Luzon led by the Communist Party of the Philippines, which had for years been mobilizing poor peasants against the domination of the countryside by a landowning oligarchy (Wurfel, 1982). This class of landowners represented a style of feudalism reminiscent of Latin America, with absentee landlords share-cropping their paddy and corn lands and exercising feudal non-market power over the lives of their tenants, who were kept in line by private armies. Ownership of land tended to be concentrated in the paddy lands, but nowhere near the level prevalent in Latin America or even Pakistan. Thus in Luzon, 328 landowners controlled 50,000 hectares or 8% of paddy lands in 1960, but even here only 1,042 holdings exceeded 50 hectares (King, 1977). Outside the paddy lands, capitalist *haciendas* engaged in cultivating sugar-cane and other commercial crops co-existed with the feudalism prevailing in the paddy lands.

This feudal class, along with the capitalist *hacendados*, dominated the legislature and frustrated attempts to realize any reform which would disturb their power in the countryside. The Marcos agrarian reform was in this sense designed to break the power of this class, but not so much to emancipate the peasantry as to frustrate any challenge to his autocracy (Wurfel, 1982).

The reforms sought to eliminate share tenancy as a relation of production by making tenants into owners of the land they cultivated, and the idea was presumably to create a class of peasant proprietors. On the eve of the reform in 1971, owner-operated and managed farms accounted for 58% of farms in the paddy and corn lands, and covered 63% of the agricultural area (Sobhan, 1983). The 11% of the households farming 11% of the land were classified as part-owners. Thus 31% of farms operating 26% of the lands were classified as pure tenants. A presidential decree enacted in 1972 sought to place all tenanted rice and corn lands in holdings above seven hectares within the purview of the reform. This law was subsequently modified under pressure from a large constituency of middle-class absentee landowners to permit all landowners with holdings between seven and 24 hectares to retain seven hectares. This class accounted for 11–15% of all landowners; 89% were described as absentee and

64% stated that they had no other occupation and depended for 88% of their income on their leased lands. Tenants on the seven hectares of land retained by the owners, along with those tenants who were leasing land from owners with holdings of below seven hectares, were to be given permanent and inheritable leasehold rights on their holdings on very favourable terms.

The total area identified for recovery under the reform came to 1.5 million hectares. The total number of landlords with share tenants came to as many as 484,430. Of these 49,221, 10.2% of the total, were liable to surrender title to 730,734 acres or about 50% of the total paddy and corn area covered by the reform. Some 396,000 share tenants or 39% of the total number of tenants were to become owners of their land. The remaining 61% of the share tenants were to remain as permanent leaseholders on 732,000 hectares of land owned by 435,000 small landowners.

It is significant that the reform thus retained tenancy on over half of paddy and corn lands and three-fifths of cultivating households remained tenants. At the same time the reform excluded from its coverage all lands under commercial crops, the principal of which were sugar-cane and coconut. These numbered 859,000 or 36.5% of all farms, which occupied 4.3 million hectares or 51.1% of all agricultural land. Thus in effect the reform converted only 16.8% of all farm households into owner-cultivators and gave them title to 8.6% of all agricultural land (Sobhan, 1983).

The reform left untouched the large constituency of landless agricultural labourers; in 1982 there were some 3.4 million landless households, of which 2.4 million worked on paddy and corn lands (Ledesma, 1982). This large underclass of the peasantry also worked on the lands of the new land reform beneficiaries.

The Filipino agrarian reform was instrumental in eliminating a dominant class of powerful *hacendados* which controlled the lives of a large number of share-croppers on paddy and corn lands. This landed gentry, however, reconstituted itself in the rural townships where its control of the credit, inputs and commodity market made it a powerful influence in rural life. The big landowners who had links with the urban economy survived as part of the urban capitalist class. The land reform beneficiaries, both the amortizing owners and the permanent leaseholders, undoubtedly faced an enhancement in their social authority with improved security of tenure, and to that extent the balance of power in village life was modified even though share-cropping remained an important factor in rural life.

Capitalism in the countryside remained untouched however, and a class of *hacendados*, both foreign and native with large plantations in sugar-cane, bananas, pineapple, even in corporate rice farms, with investments in cattle ranches and with downstream investments in agro-industry, hiring wage labour and entering into contract farming arrangements with smallholders adjacent to them, remain a powerful social and political force not only in the countryside but also in national life (Sobhan, 1983). In the coconut sector alone, some 500,000 share-croppers and 1,000,000 hired labourers remain dependent on a class of landowners ranging from large capitalist holdings to small tenanted farms. Agrarian reform in the Philippines, therefore, whilst having some impact on social life, has perpetuated wide differentiations in the countryside and left a large and growing underclass of landless agrarian workers outside the purview of the reform.

Monsoon Asia: comparisons and contrasts in agrarian transition

The process of agrarian reform in South-East Asia has discernible parallels with the South Asian experience. They both have the shared feature of a large class of peasant holdings cultivating small parcels of land with family labour. Share-cropping in both regions has persisted as a survival mechanism for minifundist farmers seeking to rent in land. In India, Pakistan, Bangladesh and the Philippines, agrarian reform has largely eliminated a class of large absentee landowners or superior tenure-holders who exercised feudal power over the tenants in the countryside. However the agrarian reforms never cut deep enough to eliminate even partially differentiation in the countryside, so that varying inequalities in the ownership of land and, with the exception of Thailand, a sizeable landless population characterize Monsoon agriculture in these Asian countries. The green revolution has, however, contributed to a process of agrarian transition by which, throughout these countries, landlords and rich peasants have evolved into capitalist farmers and have even modified the tenancy system to take advantage of the new technology. Thus market forces hold together the system of capitalist farming and share-cropping in these Asian countries. It may therefore be inappropriate to classify these countries of Monsoon Asia as having effected a transition to capitalist agriculture as in Latin America. But the penetration of market forces, even within relations of production associated with share-cropping, and the ubiquity of wage labour in most peasant households, suggests that the characteristics of a capitalist system are now widely manifest in Asian agriculture.

The main point of difference between South and South-East Asia lies in the more egalitarian distribution of non-corporate farm holdings. This reflects an initial more equitable pattern of holdings in Indonesia and Thailand and even the Philippines, and the relatively more successful reforms in the Philippines, at least on paddy and corn lands. The South Asian agrarian reforms were founded on a much more inequitable pattern of ownership and the influence of non-market relations in defining landlord–tenant relations was much more deeply embedded in the agrarian system. It was thus not surprising that the agrarian reforms remained, with the exception of the 1972–77 reforms in Sri Lanka, modest in conception and inordinately weak in implementation, and have left intact a much more clearly articulated degree of class differentiation in the countryside than in South-East Asia.

Africa: decolonization and agrarian reform within a capitalist mode

In North and sub-Saharan Africa we have seen that the best cultivable land had been owned and operated by colonial settlers and the decolonization process therefore had implications for the relations of production in the agrarian system of these countries. We have already discussed the impact of decolonization in Algeria, Mozambique and Angola where the settlers' departure was quite abrupt and thus had an effect on the post-colonial agrarian system. In the three cases briefly discussed below the colonial withdrawal was more gradual and could thus be effected without immediately disturbing the relation of production in agriculture. The cases to be reviewed cover Tunisia in North Africa, which was under French rule, and Kenya and Zimbabwe, both of which were under British rule (although after the unilateral declaration of independence by its white settler-dominated administration in 1967, Zimbabwe was under white settler rule).

Kenya: building a capitalist agriculture

The white settler withdrawal from Kenya was one of the most gradual in the post-colonial world, and is still not complete a quarter of a century after independence. At independence in 1961, European settlements in the Kenyan highlands covered 30,000 square kilometres (King, 1977). These settlements were family- or corporate-run capitalist enterprises which dominated the country's agricultural and export economy. The lands were reserved for white settlement and the exclusion of the indigenous population from what were deemed to be their ancestral lands had triggered off the Mau Mau rebellion of the 1950s.

Land access for Africans in the Kenyan highlands was one of the principal goals of agrarian reform in post-independence Kenya. The aim of the Kenyan government was progressively to acquire the surplus lands of the settlers for redistribution to African families to cultivate as medium-sized family farms. However the Kenyan government also wanted the white settlers to continue to run their capitalist farms, which remained the main source of production and exports from the farm sector. Around 400,000 hectares were acquired between 1963 and 1967 to settle 35,000 smallholder families in 3,000–4,000 farm settlements, each covering about 4,000 hectares with each family being assigned 10–13 hectares. By the late 1960s some 800 European estates covering nearly half a million hectares had been broken into about 40,000 small-holdings. This suggests that some of these newly created holdings were fairly sizeable, and indicated an attempt to create, along with the family farm, a class of African capitalist farmers. This pattern of settlement involving fairly liberal access to land was designed to leave relations of production undisturbed. It meant, however, that only 3% of farming families in Kenya received land under the reforms. A strategy of creating private tenures and some element of a capitalist agriculture was thus bound to create severe inequalities in access to land in a society where the tribal system provided access for most people seeking to cultivate land (Hunt, 1984). Given the high rate of population growth in Kenya, the strategy of creating a capitalist agriculture is contributing to a growing class of landless rural households who have to be absorbed as wage labourers on the private holdings. The incapacity of private agriculture to do so has meant that urban migration and poverty are the product of the strategy of creating a class of private tenure-holders (Hunt, 1984).

Zimbabwe: a not dissimilar path?

The Kenyan experience was paralleled in post-liberation Zimbabwe. As in Kenya, white settlers in Zimbabwe dominated the best lands which were reserved exclusively for them, and operated large-scale capitalist farms employing wage labour. In 1969 such farms accounted for 40% of the agricultural land (Cliffe, 1986). In contrast, the majority black population controlled the less fertile 41.5% of the land which was tilled largely under various forms of communal tenure. A small proportion of the land, about 3.5%, was held in small-scale commercial farms operated by Africans within tribal lands. The usufruct of the land was relatively more equitably distributed, largely in holdings of 1–5 hectares (about 50%) and 6–10 hectares (about 25–30%). Holdings above 10 hectares were rare and landlessness was also low, varying between 6 and 11% in different regions.

It was an article of faith with the Zimbabwean liberation forces that at independence white settler lands should be opened to settlement by the Africans subsisting on marginal lands. Despite the protracted and violent character of the liberation struggle, the evolution to majority rule in Zimbabwe came through a negotiated constitutional settlement which protected white settler lands and committed the new government to pay compensation for white lands it acquired. While some white settlers abandoned their farms and left the country, most stayed on and some of those who fled the country at the time of independence returned when they accepted that the new Zimbabwean government was likely to operate within the limits of the negotiated constitutional arrangement guaranteeing white settlers security of property.

Within the constitutional constraints inherited by the first black government in Zimbabwe, there was not much scope for a major land reform, but there was scope to buy out white settlers and to bring unused lands under cultivation. Thus abandoned farms were taken over and surplus lands under white settler farms were resumed by the state, with payment of compensation. This was designated for distribution to the African landless and land-poor. Under these two components of the land reform programme some 2.5 million hectares were resumed by the government in the first five years after independence. Two million hectares have since been distributed to 35,000 peasant families assembled in 50 settlement schemes. Some of these schemes are run as collective farms, but most are set up as family farms. Their size suggests that some of these farms hire in labour and constitute small capitalist farms. By 1984 some 18% of the land held by white settlers had been redistributed to Africans.

The 'socialist' commitment of the Zimbabwean government has meant that the process of creating a class of African capitalists, as in Kenya, was likely to make much less headway, even though large-scale white capitalist farms continued to dominate the countryside. Given the large proportion of lands available in Zimbabwe, the initial strategy is one of resettlement of the landless without disturbing productive white farms. The hope is that this new class does not become a pocket of poverty and arrested development. Resettlement is, however, a capital-intensive task given the need to make once arid lands productive and to provide working capital and services to the newly settled African farmers.

The crucial issue will arise with the withdrawal of the bulk of the white settlers and the tenurial arrangements to govern newly acquired lands. Given the move towards at least a *de facto* one party state in Zimbabwe and the Mugabe government's amendment of the constitution to end the special protection assigned to both the vote and lands of white settlers, the hold of most settlers appears somewhat uncertain. In this event crucial decisions governing the tenurial arrangements governing access to land will be in order. The appropriate mode of production which will develop in Zimbabwe will thus emerge from the ideological character and political direction of the contemporary Zimbabwean government.

Tunisia: contradictions

In Tunisia decolonization was a more gradual process. The French *colon* presence in Tunisia was no less strong than in Algeria, with 6,600 *colon* holdings controlling 18% of the most fertile lands and contributing 40% of agricultural output (King, 1977). This again prevented the emergence of an indigenous feudal class, though a class of indigenous capitalist farmers, encouraged by the *colons'* successes, was present. In contrast to Algeria, the moderate direction of state policy in post-independence Tunisia led to Tunisian and French capitalism co-existing. However political conflicts with France, influenced by the winds of radical nationalism in the neighbouring North African states, drove the Tunisian government to expedite the take-over of French lands already begun on a modest scale after independence. Thus in 1964 a decree nationalizing all foreign-owned landholdings effectively placed 805,000 hectares, 38% of all cultivable land, under state ownership.

As in Algeria, the less radical Tunisian government opted to go for a form of state ownership rather than to redistribute the integrated *colon* holdings to local capitalists or even to tenant cultivators. This extension of the state sector, however, continued to co-exist with a class of indigenous capitalist farmers. This class effectively frustrated the extension of land reforms as took place in Algeria a decade after independence. Thus by 1970 only 218 farms, employing 10,000 wage workers, remained in the state sector. These farmed only 203,000 hectares, which accounted for 9.6% of all cultivable land in Tunisia. The prospect of a limited form of capitalist agriculture co-existing with small holdings is thus characteristic of Tunisia compared to the dominant presence of the state sector, co-operatives and more equitably held private lands in neighbouring Algeria.

Decolonization and class formation: the dilemma of agrarian reform in Africa
We may thus attempt to summarize the impact of external intervention and its withdrawal on the process of agrarian relations in Africa by viewing it in relation to the impact it has on the development of indigenous class forces. Where the external presence had an impact on the internal balance of forces in the countryside, as it did in parts of sub-Saharan and North Africa, it frustrates the emergence of a dominant indigenous landed class. A precipitate withdrawal leads to the dominance of the state in the agricultural sector, usually through various forms of state, collective or co-operative tenurial arrangements. Where withdrawals are less precipitate, an indigenous capitalist class may, however, evolve from the class of richer farmers (in the Kenyan case as a result of conscious state policy) but this new class will not exercise the social dominance associated with a long-established landed elite.

6. The Economic Impact of Agrarian Reform

CONCEPTUAL ISSUES

Problems of estimating the economic impact of reforms

In discussing the impact of agrarian reforms we have already reviewed the socio-political circumstances and outcome of such reforms and have attempted to relate the political context of reforms to their social outcome in a variety of countries throughout the world. To trace the economic impact of such reforms therefore presupposes that an agrarian reform is of a sufficient dimension to have a cumulative impact on the national economy as distinct from an impact on the household of a land reform beneficiary. This distinction is important because the ultimate rationale of agrarian reforms tends to be built around its contribution to social transformation, agricultural growth and economic development. To say that vesting land on landless households or easing the terms of tenancy for share-croppers would improve their economic circumstances would be something of a truism.

In the short run the retained output of the land reform beneficiary may be partly or entirely in amortization payments to the erstwhile landlord or the state, depending on the nature and terms on which lands under the reform have been appropriated and assigned to the land reform beneficiary. The access to this particular benefit thus depends quite clearly on the terms of the reform which in turn derive from the nature of the reforms. Whatever the immediate welfare gain for the land reform beneficiary, it will have to be set against the opportunity costs of severing the tenants' link with the landlord in related factor markets other than land, which provides access to credits, inputs, water, extension services and protection/mediation in relation to the machinery of state. If all or part of such services are indeed provided by the landlord, the land reform beneficiary will have to substitute these services at lower opportunity cost from other sources, be they in the open market or the state. Failure to do so at all, in part or at the same cost as that provided by the landlord could erode part or all of the gains from retaining the crop share hitherto surrendered to the landlord.

Where the land reform beneficiary had no links at all to a landlord but was, *ab initio*, without access to land, all such services indicated above will be identified as direct costs to the land reform beneficiary which will have to be met before he can generate a return from the newly acquired land. For the landless, the net return from the land will have to be measured against the opportunity cost of the land reform beneficiary's labour sold on the open market. This cost will have to be computed in terms of the prevailing wage rate and days of employment provided by the market. If the returns from the land are indeed insufficient to meet the opportunity cost of labour, then the economic benefits from reform may not be immediately apparent to a land reform beneficiary.

Whilst the immediate costs and benefits from being given access to land or improved tenure terms can be estimated in terms of household income and expenditure, the intangible gains from increased intensity of labour input on owned land is less evident but certainly open to estimation. Household level micro-analysis of the impact of agrarian reform can thus possibly measure the immediate impact of such reforms. Available research methodology for analysing the impact of a reform makes even such obvious evaluations problematic, and screening out all other variables influencing household income to isolate the specific contribution of the reform has never been satisfactorily accomplished. The use of micro-survey techniques based on control areas where the reform has taken place, and non-control areas which have not benefited from reform, suffer from the difficulty of controlling all other variables or establishing equivalence in the circumstances of the control and non-control area. The use of base-line surveys at the outset of the reform to provide comparisons of the beneficiaries' circumstances before and after the reform remains somewhat more reliable than the use of control and non-control survey areas. But even here the difficulties of controlling for social changes over time in the land reform area again make it difficult conclusively to establish the precise contribution of agrarian reforms.

Studies in the Philippines of land reform beneficiaries' households on the specific impact of the 1972 reforms provide no categorical evidence on the immediate impact of the reforms, though some studies do suggest short-term gains in household income. However there are other studies which, conversely, point to a depreciation in real terms of land reform beneficiaries' household income, which suggests that over a long time period the reform made no discernible impact on the circumstances of the beneficiaries (Mangahas et al., 1976). Other studies of Latin American agrarian reforms generate similar agnosticism about the impact of the reforms at the household level (World Bank, 1978).

There will, of course, be a large number of cases where assignment of land to pure landless or land-poor households with insufficient access to employment in the labour market will effect a visible improvement in their circumstances, though much less so than may have been at the outset argued by the protagonists of the reform. In such circumstances the net gains of such a reform may be assessed in relation to access to employment provided by the market rather than the net gains to various factors of production where indeed both land and labour remain underutilized. Thus in Guatemala for instance, in 1954, at the time of the Arbenz agrarian reforms, land redistribution of hitherto unutilized land would have had an unambiguously positive impact (Schlesinger and Kinzer, 1983).

The actual impact of a reform on household income may thus be expected to vary greatly both between communities and households. The extent to which the state commits itself to regulate the factor markets for capital, inputs and output, whilst investing in infrastructure to help land reform beneficiaries, will have a significant impact on households, particularly where this intervention is not territorially uniform. The flexibility of factor markets to cope at least cost with the new structure of demand emanating from the land reform beneficiary, as indeed the behaviour of product markets in the aftermath of the reform, may be no less significant in its impact on the land reform beneficiary. Finally, the varying circumstances of the land reform beneficiary in relation to the quality and stock of household labour and access to capital, not to mention the entrepreneurial resources of the household, will all influence the beneficiaries.

The available micro-level studies on the impact of agrarian reforms on the circumstances of individual households do not generate enough confidence on the distinctive contribution of such reforms *per se* on the fortunes of particular households. It is thus more useful to trace at a macro-level the coincidence of such reforms with increments in agricultural productivity, improvements in employment opportunities and living standards and in the generation and mobilization of reinvestible surpluses from the agricultural sector. Some changes may not originate directly from agrarian reforms. The changes do, however, derive from a policy environment conducive to such improvements in economic performance, where agrarian reform is perhaps the most important but not the sole influence. It follows from our perspective articulated in Chapter 2 that the correlation of social forces necessary to bring about an agrarian reform would have an impact on the agricultural economy. In this section we will therefore focus our analysis on reviewing the chain of causality which links agrarian reform with economic performance.

The causal link between agrarian reforms and economic change

The causal link between changes in the macro-economy and agrarian reform may briefly be examined. Increases in agricultural production must presumably originate in improvements in land productivity and expansion in the area under cultivation. Expansion of the cultivable area is most relevant to the circumstances in Latin America, where the latifundia system tended to keep large areas of land untilled. To the extent that agrarian reform brings in peasants from outside the *haciendas*, or increases lands reserved for the plantation sector at the disposal of the *colonatos* who are confined to the marginal lands of the *hacienda*, there would be a presumption that such land would be more intensively used after the reform. This assumption would not hold good where the untilled areas of the *haciendas* can only be tilled after considerable investment in the land by way of clearance, levelling and the provision of irrigation.

In the Middle East, Africa and even in India and Pakistan, land hitherto vested in large holdings could not effectively be reclaimed without substantial investments. It is no accident that lands surrendered under ceiling legislation, whether in Latin America, the Middle East or Asia, usually tended to be uncultivated and possibly uncultivable in the absence of sufficient investment. Even in much of Monsoon Asia, where there is very little uncultivated land, scope for enhancing the cultivable area and indeed the productive capacity of the land may require sizeable investments in land improvement and irrigation.

In the absence of such investments by the state in land development, at the margin, the principal route to enhancing land productivity must be through enhanced investment of household labour. The contribution of land reform to this increased use of household labour would be through the incentive provided to the land reform beneficiary from ownership of land and the right to the fruits of his labour invested in the land. Obviously incremental investments of labour presume that the household has sufficient under-employed labour to deploy on the land. This scope for more intensive use of household labour by land reform beneficiaries would be measured in terms of fuller employment and enhanced returns from the land. This would imply not only higher household income but a higher volume of national agricultural output derived from fuller utilization at the margin of both land and labour.

The link between land reform and utilization of untilled land is, however, not easy to establish empirically except through isolated case studies (World Bank, 1978), but it has been established that land held in smallholdings is more fully utilized than in large holdings (Berry and Cline, 1979). This is hardly surprising given that man/land ratios on small farms would be conducive to fuller land use. But this remains a general characteristic of small farms which exist independent of land reforms. Thus the evidence at hand may provide an argument for reform but can hardly be used to measure its outcome.

A further measure of the impact of agrarian reforms on the agricultural economy may be seen in that the extent to which cropping patterns also undergo some changes towards more land- and labour-intensive crops and/or from pasture to arable farming, the change in cropping patterns would reflect a restructuring of aggregate agricultural output away from export-oriented cash crop/livestock farming towards subsistence food production. To this end this move may enhance output but reduce the total value of agricultural output as well as reduce foreign exchange earned from agriculture. It would at the margin also substitute savings for current consumption. These substitutions, of course, could be moderated by disproportionate increments in productivity amongst land reform beneficiaries which could make up through import substitution what is lost in export earnings. Conversely, economies of scale in capitalist farming of export crops may be quite inadequately compensated for by enhanced output for home consumption, and the loss in savings and export earnings may have a cumulative effect on the national economy.

The possibility that agrarian reform cuts into the agricultural surplus has remained a perennial concern of its critics. It was argued, particularly in the Soviet context in the 1920s, that by withdrawing land from big capitalist farmers who produce for the market or landlords who market the crop share yielded up by the tenant, and by distributing the land to minifundist farmers whose incremental investments of labour will merely raise levels of production from sub-subsistence to subsistence levels, there will be a deterioration in the level of savings, investment and eventual growth of the national economy. The only way in which the diseconomies of subsistence farming and the erosion of the marketed surplus can be compensated is through the conversion of subsistence-level household cultivation into producer co-operatives or collective farms from which the agricultural surplus can be collectively appropriated (Dobb, 1941).

The chain of causality between agrarian reforms and macro-economic performance can rarely be linear given the variables other than reform which tend to influence this performance. Changes in cropping pattern, land use, yield and surplus generation may be influenced by changes in the market place, public policy interventions influencing the market regime and productive capacity. Thus the fate of post-reform agriculture tends to depend as much, if not more, on contingent developments in the national and global economy and the society as it does on the reform itself.

Agricultural policies and the economic impact of agrarian reforms

It would therefore be appropriate to identify the attendant policy and market variables associated with the reform which could affect agricultural performance. In developing our analysis we will, by way of illustration, draw upon the agrarian reform experiences of some of the countries discussed in Chapter 3.

Policy interventions tend to be far from neutral and reflect the balance of social forces which influence the direction of state policy. To the extent that we have argued that the intent and scope of an agrarian reform derives from this balance of forces, the corresponding thrust of related policies will reflect this same balance of forces. Where a reform derives from a change in the balance of forces towards strengthening the poor peasantry, agrarian reforms have been more radical in their distributive impact.

Agrarian reform in the context of a bias against agriculture

It may be presumed that a regime sensitive to the needs of poor peasants would back up its agrarian reform with support in related markets for credit, inputs, extension services, in its pricing regime and its allocative priorities. However this association need not always be so, and it is possible that a regime which has carried through radical reforms on the land may continue to address its allocative priorities to the urban sector. This is more likely to happen where the political support for the regime comes from both the urban and the rural poor so that the deflection of priorities from the rural to the urban sector may not reflect a class-biased perspective but a manifestation of inter-temporal priorities between sectors. Thus it may be argued that the initial direction of public resources and the manipulation of the terms of trade against agriculture may be dictated by the need to accelerate capital accumulation so that growth, saving and reinvestment may be speeded up.

It is important to spell out the assumptions underlying an anti-rural bias in allocative strategies because it is quite feasible to argue for a rate of rapid accumulation based on investments in the agricultural sector. The con-commitant increase in agricultural output could be translated into exports which generate the foreign currency needed to import capital goods to sustain the process of accumulation and diversification of the economic structure. The original argument must therefore presume that there is some finite limit to the overseas market's ability to absorb agricultural exports so that at the margin an inward direction to the process of accumulation is necessary to provide sufficient autonomy to the process of reproduction within the economy.

It is significant that all the countries identified by us in Chapter 3 as having effected radical redistributive reforms have tended to be supportive of the agricultural sector in the post-reform phase. In contrast, the radical reforms carried through, initially in the USSR and subsequently in Eastern Europe, have been accused of being much less sensitive to the agricultural sector in the allocative priorities (Lewin, 1968). This blanket perspective may have some exceptions such as Bulgaria, but tends to be associated with the Soviet model of accumulation linked with Stalin although having its intellectual origins in Preobrazhensky's theories (Mitra, 1979). It is, of course, arguable that initially neither Stalin nor Preobrazhensky argued that agriculture should be a less privileged sector of the economy. Their presumption was that the accelerated accumulation process would in the second phase generate a stream of investment goods such as tractors and combine harvesters which would permit the modernization of agriculture and the improvement of agricultural productivity and household incomes. Since the agricultural sector provided the principal source of export earnings and the principal wage goods available for purchase by factory workers in the capital goods sector, agricultural workers would in this initial period have to surrender their surplus without immediate compensation in the form of manufactured consumer goods or indeed capital goods. Here again, the idea was to divert the surplus and not to cut into current consumption of the peasant sector.

The collectivization of agriculture in the USSR became an essential element in this strategy since the market mechanism could not stimulate the flow of the agricultural surplus to the export and urban sectors without a return flow of manufactured wage goods, and merely led to an adverse movement in the terms of trade against agriculture which resulted in the drying up of the exportable surplus from agriculture (Dobb, 1948). Collectivization sought to institutionalize access to the agricultural surplus by providing physical control over the surplus and its unrequited diversion to the urban sector.

The purely economic compulsion underlying the drive towards collectivization in the USSR under Stalin was, of course, sustained by Lenin's notions of class struggle (Mitra, 1979). Preobrazhensky, who also claimed to draw his inspiration from Lenin, associated private control over the agricultural surplus with the kulaks who had prospered under the New Economic Policy (NEP). This class, operating within the market mechanism, tended to generate and control the agricultural surplus and was reluctant to surrender it to the state unless it was compensated through acceptable prices which established equivalence in exchange between agriculture and industry. If this equivalence was not established in the market, the kulaks could withhold supplies for local consumption and could eventually reduce production. The attempt to appropriate the agricultural surplus through the system of non-equivalent exchange, as argued by Preobrazhensky, thus demanded that the kulaks be either brought under control or eliminated as a class by a transformation in the relations of production (Mitra, 1979). This implies that the institution of private accumulation of the surplus through cultivation of land by individual households would have to be transformed into the collective generation, accumulation and appropriation of the surplus.

However, collectivization of production in itself need not provide a basis for non-equivalent exchange since a collective of farmers could be quite as sensitive to market forces governing the terms of exchange for their surplus and no less inclined to withhold it for domestic consumption within the collective than a kulak who retained the surplus for household consumption. Thus the notion of farmer's autonomy associated with collective farming had to co-exist with the unarticulated assumption that the state would dictate the terms of exchange with the agricultural sector, be it under private ownership or collectivized. This implies that the state commands the capacity to suppress democratic expressions of opinion, particularly in societies where a plurality may consist of households depending on agriculture for their livelihood. In this context the dictatorship of the proletariat could thus quite easily come to mean the dictatorship of the urban proletariat, at least for that period of time when non-equivalent exchange remained the principal instrument of socialist accumulation.

It is obvious that agrarian reform is thus no guarantee of a transformation in the circumstances of the peasantry if it has to surrender the surplus from its newly titled lands under non-equivalent terms of exchange. Collectivization thus becomes a convenient mechanism for more readily socializing this surplus and making it more accessible to the state. Under private ownership it is immeasurably more difficult for the state to control the production, consumption and marketing decisions of large numbers of scattered households, as became only too apparent under the NEP (Dobb, 1948). Collectivization was thus needed to dictate the production targets and the surplus to be surrendered by the members of the collective. Production shortfalls could thus be compensated by cut-backs in consumption within the collective rather than through an erosion of the surplus to be surrendered to the state.

The contrary case

It is argued that a strategy of accumulation based on the appropriation of the surplus of the land reform beneficiaries is only feasible if the revolution does not originate within the peasantry and is less sensitive to their concerns. The notion of the state imposing sacrifices of current consumption on a majority of farm households is much less feasible where state power is itself underwritten by a mobilized peasantry which played a vanguard role in the revolution creating the socialist state. This particular hypothesis is consistent with the divergent strategies in the European and Asian socialist states towards the peasantry. The Asian socialist revolutions, and even the Cuban revolution, drew their support from poor peasants and thus felt compelled to direct their pricing and allocative policies to bring about a discernible improvement in the peasants' circumstances. This meant that the burden of accumulation did not have to be carried by the agricultural sector.

In fairness, however, it must be said that China, North Korea and North Vietnam did not have to go through the process of autonomous accumulation forced upon the USSR in the peculiar circumstances in which it found itself in the 1920s and 1930s as the only socialist state. The Asian socialist states and Cuba could draw upon the resources of the European socialist states, and particularly on the USSR, in the immediate aftermath of their revolutions, in contributing to the process of accumulation and facilitating the structural transformation of their domestic economies. When China was forced to follow the Soviet path of autonomous accumulation following its break with the USSR in the early 1960s it already had a well developed industrial sector and a substantial capital goods sector built up in the 1950s, largely with the assistance of the USSR. In contrast the young USSR was cut off from sources of external financing and, as much by necessity as choice, had not only to go for a strategy of internal accumulation but to accelerate this process to be able to withstand the strategy of encirclement which it believed the capitalist world was pursuing in order, to quote Winston Churchill, 'to destroy the Bolshevik beast in its lair'.

THE ECONOMIC IMPACT OF RADICAL AGRARIAN REFORM IN EGALITARIAN ECONOMIES

Policies to support the post-reform agricultural sector

This digression on the approach to agriculture in the post-reform phase of the socialist states is designed to show that a transformation in relations of production needs to be coterminous with a transformation in the fortunes of a post-reform peasantry, the sources of power underwriting the change in the domestic balance of power and the changes being reflected as a result in a constellation of supportive domestic policies designed to assist the land reform beneficiaries. In this respect the radical reforms of the socialist world shared the same perspective with the East Asian reformers in Japan, South Korea and Taiwan. We may, therefore, attempt to look at the policy regime of these seven countries and the relation between these policies and the performance of their respective agricultural sectors.

All four socialist countries pursued pricing policies designed to provide incentives to producers, subsidized the price of inputs, provided liberal access to institutional credit, provided efficient extension services and institutionalized support for marketing their produce. All four states invested heavily in irrigation, roads, housing, public health and education and other areas of the rural infrastructure.

Such a policy and allocative regime characterized the four socialist economies. These interventions were supplemented by fiscal and pricing policies which were either supportive of the peasantry, or at least not discriminatory. In the case of China, for example, the tax burden on agriculture in terms of the compulsory procurement by the state was much less exacting than in the USSR (Nolan, 1982). Thus in China it was estimated that the net extraction rate of grains from agriculture declined from 17.1% in 1953–54 to 11.3% in 1957–58. In contrast, the rate of grain procurement in the USSR increased from 14.7% in the pre-collectivization phase in 1928 to 33% in 1933.

Similarly in the area of pricing policy, the terms of trade between agriculture and industry in China consistently moved in favour of agriculture in the aftermath of the reform between 1950 and 1958, in contrast to the USSR where collectivization led to a deterioration in agriculture's terms of trade (Nolan, 1982). It is argued by Nolan that the policy compulsion to stimulate increases in grain output in China in the post-reform phase was dictated by unusually low levels of grain output, which stood at 270 kilograms per capita in 1951, while in the USSR the compulsion was to generate a grain surplus for promoting industrial accumulation since the level of agricultural production was much higher compared to China. Indeed, in the USSR in 1932 during the hard days of collectivization, 375 kilograms per capita was left for consumption within the farm sector after extracting 27% of the grain surplus.

In Cuba, agriculture became something of a privileged sector. Even though agriculture's share of the GDP declined to 18% in 1981, public investment in the sector rose from 29.4% of the total in 1962 to 40.4% in 1966, and even in 1981 accounted for 27.2% of public investment (Brundenius, 1984). Thus investment per head of the agricultural labour force in 1981 came to 1,254 pesos compared to 905 pesos for the non-agricultural sector. Cuba must indeed be one of the few developing countries to use its development expenditure in favour of the agricultural sector.

In the case of Vietnam much less is known about the policies pursued to support land reform beneficiaries. Any attempt to link the reforms with allocative policies and benefits to the peasants has to make allowances for the destruction and dislocation effected by the war against French colonialism in the 1950s and then against the United States between 1965 and 1975. This second war not only claimed resources which would have been invested in development but heavily damaged the economy's infrastructure and productive capacity. The aftermath of this was felt in South Vietnam after its unification with the North in 1975. The South had in fact been in a state of virtually continuous social and physical dislocation since the anti-Japanese struggle in the 1940s which was aggravated by the fact that for nearly 15 years the rural areas of the South were the theatre of a major war.

Despite the effects of the anti-French war in the aftermath of agrarian reform in North Vietnam, state investment in agriculture and credits to the farmers increased by 96.4% between 1955–57 and 1958–60 (Ministry of Agriculture, 1986). Both state and local investment in water control raised the irrigated area in North Vietnam to 60% of the cultivated area by 1960 (Ministry of Agriculture, 1986). Between 1960 and 1975, some 198 million cubic metres of dykes were built in the North. This was reinforced by a major increase in the provision of fertilizer and pesticides to farmers. Such investments may not have led to a major improvement in the standard of living, but they were equitably distributed, involved considerable mobilization of domestic resources, including labour, and could relate the reforms and the mobilization of resources directly to the welfare of the peasants.

Data on the policies and commitment of resources to the agricultural sector in North Korea remain much more obscure. The North Korean model much more closely followed the early Soviet model of autarchic development, but this seems to have been without prejudice to the agricultural sector. Before the war the South had been the bread-basket of a unified Korea, so one of the post-war goals of the regime in North Korea was to attain self-reliance in foodstuffs through the rapid modernization of agriculture. This required massive investment in irrigation, which covered 37,000 kilometres of earthworks, the electrification of rural areas and the use of 80,000 tractors, which gives North Korea one of the highest tractor/cultivable land ratios in the developing world (McCormack and Gittings, 1977). Chemical fertilizer use increased from 15 kilograms per hectare in 1970 to 345 kilograms – which was exceeded in the developing world in countries with a significant agricultural sector only by Egypt (World Bank, 1987, Table 6).

This supportive regime towards agriculture is much more fully documented for the East Asian economies of Japan, Taiwan and South Korea and does not require any further description here. By way of illustration, in South Korea public expenditure on agriculture increased 3.6 times in real terms between 1969–74 and 1983–84 (Sobhan, 1986). In a measure developed by the writer to test public expenditure priorities to agriculture in relation to the share of agriculture in the GDP, South Korea has one of the more favourable ratings in the developing world (Sobhan, 1986). Pricing policies have also been favourable. Between 1973 and 1983 prices rose consistently for both cereal crops (77%) and major export crops (51%). The terms of trade between fertilizer and crop prices was one of the most favourable in the developing world, and these favourable terms of trade applied to sectoral terms of trade as well. Agriculture was, in fact, a subsidized sector of the economy, and a net recipient of resources. This support for the farm sector was, however, not always the case and reflects a change in the direction of public policy in the 1960s after a period of neglect in the 1950s in the immediate aftermath of agrarian reform. South Korea is in fact a case in point where the correlation between the agrarian reforms and a policy regime supportive of small farmers took over a decade to fall into alignment.

The point in common between the socialist and East Asian economies, originating in the highly egalitarian nature of their respective agrarian reforms, is that the benefits from all such policy and allocative interventions of the state tends to be equitably and directly distributed within the village community. The residual class of landlords and rich farmers who survived or grew out of the land reforms in other countries, to become leaders of the community and mediators for state-provided resources, has been socially uprooted in these countries, so the unequal incidence of benefits in the rural economy from public policy and allocations could be avoided. In these circumstances the incentive as well as scope for enhanced land and household productivity could be coterminous with improvements in household incomes and living standards and the rapid eradication of the extreme forms of rural poverty which characterized the pre-reform society in these countries and continues to afflict other developing countries.

Agricultural production trends

The favourable trend in government policies towards agriculture is reflected in the positive trends in agricultural production in all seven countries.

In China grain production increased at the rate of 5.7% a year between 1949 and 1954 and 4.5% between 1953 and 1957 (Wong, 1973). In the first decade after the 1949 land reform and the subsequent collectivization of agriculture, food production increased from an index of 93 in 1949–52 to 163 in 1959 (Wong, 1973), well above the average for all regions of the developing world during the same period. Even though considerable instability in grain production prevailed in China in the 1960s, partly due to the weather and partly to the upheavals associated first with the Great Leap Forward and then with the Cultural Revolution, total grain production tripled from 113 million tons in 1959 to 332 in 1979 (Hanxian, 1985). Correspondingly, grain yield per mou (one-sixth of an acre) increased from 68.5 kilograms in 1949 to 185.5 kilograms (Hanxian, 1985). This level of increase was also manifest in cash crops such as cotton, oil-bearing crops, jute, sugar-cane and beetroot. The value of agricultural production increased at an annual rate of 10.7% between 1949 and 1957 (Hanxian, 1985). This growth in production and productivity was reflected in a transformation in the incomes of the agricultural population whose average annual income increased from ¥ 55 in 1949 ¥ 161 in 1979 (Hanxian, 1985). This increase in disposable cash income was matched by increases in social welfare in the form of improved health, education and community facilities, not to mention the enhancement in the security and stability of rural life. This is not to say that China did not have poverty, or indeed experience privation and even famine (Sen, 1981). However such poverty, as indeed such income gains, were largely shared so that aggregating estimates of output and income growth, unlike in most developing countries, do tend to reflect changes in the circumstances of most of the rural population. Differentiation may exist between households in more and less advanced regions but much less so within regions.

The experience in China is paralleled in North Korea, although here statistics tend to be sparse. According to FAO sources, North Korea has sustained an annual rate of growth of agricultural output which puts it in the ranks of the fastest-growing of the developing countries. According to the World Bank's World Development Report (1986), North Korea's average index of food production per capita increased from 100 in 1974–76 to 113 in 1982–84. This increase in output enabled it to increase daily calorie supply per capita from 2,255 kg. in 1965 to 3,151 kg. in 1985, which is exceeded in the developing world only by Syria, Mexico, Argentina, the United Arab Emirates and Libya (World Bank, 1986, Table 28). However, whilst all these countries except Argentina sustained this level of consumption through large increases in imports of food, North Korea reduced its food imports from 1.1 million tons in 1974 to 200,000 tons in 1985 (World Bank 1986, Table 6). Furthermore, within its socialized distribution system, this high level of food consumption was likely to be shared by all households.

In the case of Vietnam, if we compare agricultural production as it existed in 1939, which was the last year of normalcy before first the anti-Japanese war and then the war against French colonialism came to disrupt the agrarian system, food production rose from 2.7 million tons in 1939 to 17.9 million tons in 1984 (Ministry of Agriculture, 1986). Per capita production rose from 228 kg. of foodgrain to 310 kg. in the same period. Rice yield also doubled from 13.04 quintals per hectare to 27.5 between 1939 and 1984. Average agricultural income per head rose from an index of 100 in 1960 to 221 in 1984.

In Cuba agricultural production appears to have declined in the immediate aftermath of the 1959 revolution averaging –0.2% per year (Brundenius, 1984). This trend, however, was reversed and growth improved speedily from 3.7% a year in 1966–70 to 3.9% in 1971–75 and 4.3% in 1976–80 and this growth rate was sustained into the 1980s. The growth in agricultural income has been realized at the same time as bringing about substantial diversification of the agricultural economy away from sugar monoculture and some cash crops. The share of non-sugar agricultural output in 1959, on the eve of the revolution, came to 44% of the total, compared to 68% in 1980. This reflected sustained growth in non-sugar crop production between 1971 and 1980 averaging 7.3% per year. Output fell in only one year, 1977, largely due to diversion of recources to increase sugar production.

There is no clearly defined measure of the improvement in agricultural incomes in Cuba, but as a proxy of this we may take national level estimates of per capita basic needs expenditure. This, in constant prices, rose from Canadian $440 in 1958 to $828 in 1980, an increase of 88% in the 22 years or around 4% a year (Brundenius, 1984 p. 179), an impressive achievement by Third World standards. To the extent that per capita agricultural output in 1979 was 1,968 pesos, almost the same as that for the total material product (i.e. GDP minus such non-productive sectors as defence), the national measure of basic needs expenditure per capita would approximate that for agriculture. Indeed agricultural sector consumption in real terms is probably higher since some of the household agricultural production for domestic consumption is not included in the national material product statistics.

The common feature of growth in agricultural production and incomes in socialist countries is that aggregate figures represent a fair proxy for the well-being of the entire rural population, since within the prevailing relations of production there is little scope for variations in household income although, as we have observed, in a country as large as China, inter-regional variations may be quite sizeable.

In the case of the East Asian economies, both productivity and agricultural household incomes improved quite appreciably in the years following their agrarian reforms. In Japan, agricultural output increased from an index of 100 to 122 in the first eight years of the reform, whilst in Taiwan it rose from 100 to 125 (Chao, 1972). These increases reflected additional use of inputs so that factor productivity increased only marginally, by 4% in both countries (Chao, 1972).

In Japan rural consumption per household increased from 100 in 1951 to 126 in 1957. In the case of Taiwan no composite index of consumption is available, but one study indicated that a diversification of consumption from basic staples to protein foods and higher value manufactured goods took place in the aftermath of the reform (Chao, 1972). Since there was also an improvement in real wages and a reduction in poverty, the reforms clearly coincided with an improvement in living standards.

The agrarian reforms in South Korea also appear to have coincided with improvements in agricultural production, land productivity, a rise in real incomes and a noticeable reduction in rural poverty. Though agricultural output increased at the rate of 2.7% between 1965 and 1973, and 1.7% between 1973 and 1984 (World Bank, 1986, Table 2), the agricultural labour force declined in absolute terms, so per capita growth rates of agricultural income grew at a much faster rate than agricultural growth rates.

Equitable access to public resources

In all three East Asian countries, as with the socialist countries discussed here, high growth rates in agriculture have been relatively equitably distributed throughout the cultivating households. This is because access to capital, inputs and public services has been distributed to all households, due largely to the absence of a differentiated class of landlords or rich peasants which could dominate rural life to the point at which it could monopolize access to public resources.

The shared experience of socialist and East Asian countries in effecting a drastic redistribution in access to land and entirely eliminating from the rural scene an incumbent or residual exploiting class, has contributed to a redirection of public policies aimed at improving the agricultural sector and, by definition, the lot of rural dwellers. Thus agricultural growth, rapid reduction of extreme poverty and an egalitarian distribution of income have emerged as features common to different modes of production. The class of beneficiaries, however, was not that dissimiliar in that the policy of ensuring that the fruits of the land were reaped directly by the tiller was a shared feature of both systems.

Structural changes in the economy

Differences in the routes taken by social transition and economic environment have nevertheless led to divergent paths achieving the same result, and in all the Asian countries in this category of radical agrarian reforms the hazards of creating minifundist production units out of a radical land reform were always present, and figured in the reformers' concerns. In China, North Korea and Vietnam, which all put emphasis on accommodating the entire class of landless and land-poor households within the compass of the reform, the economic hazards of minifundist agriculture surfaced after the reforms. This problem was, however, also manifest in South Korea where the reform left only 1.6% of households with more than three hectares of land (Rao, 1978). Taiwan and Japan effected as radical a redistribution of land as South Korea, leaving a ceiling to be retained by landlords in the region of three hectares in both countries, although in Japan a separate ceiling of 12 hectares was set for Hokkaido. Nevertheless, most holdings in Japan, South Korea and Taiwan remained about one hectare.

Diversification of the rural sector

In Japan and Taiwan, and eventually in South Korea, many of the diseconomies of small farms were compensated for by co-operative institutions for the delivery of inputs and credit and for marketing produce. This would, however, have been insufficient to sustain the pressures of demography which could have led to land fragmentation and sub-division of holdings to absorb the increased population to the point at which even co-operative services would have been inadequate to the economic viability of the minifundists.

This pressure on the land was drastically moderated in the East Asian economies by the rapid development of the non-agricultural sector within the framework of a strategy of export-led industrialization. This absorbed the increment in rural population, and indeed led to an absolute reduction in the rural labour force which further eased pressure on the land. Indeed, the growth of non-agricultural activities adjacent to the agricultural areas enabled minifundist households to seek supplementary earning opportunities outside agriculture. Thus intensive use of agricultural land together with access to non-agricultural employment raised the real earnings of the agricultural population. This development model, in which the dynamic of development is transferred to the industrial sector, made it possible for an egalitarian, minifundist peasant agriculture to survive whilst ensuring rising standards of living.

This same option was available to the Asian socialist economies such as Northern Korea and Vietnam but less so to China, given the vast rural population and difficulties of absorbing their surplus labour within the industrial sector. Again less is known of North Korea, but it is assumed that rapid industrialization did effect some structural shift in the labour force reflected in the decline in the share of the rural labour force from 57% of the total in 1965 to 43% in 1980 (World Bank, 1986, Table 30). The corresponding rise in industrial output at an annual rate of 10% in the 1950s, and the rising share of industry in North Korea's GDP from 16.8% in 1946, suggests that the development model in North Korea is not that dissimilar to that of South Korea except that in North Korea industrial growth is much less export-oriented (McCormack and Gittings, 1977).

In all three socialist countries, however, the response to the potential diseconomies arising from post-reform minifundist agriculture was seen to lie in collectivization of agriculture. The goal remained to pool land in order to ensure its more effective utilization, to optimize the use of equipment and draught animals and to provide the basis for some improvement in mechanization. More to the point, however, was the scope for using surplus labour, not fully absorbable in agriculture, in developing the social infrastructure of the village economy, particularly in labour-intensive investment projects. In China a rising proportion of household labour time of the rural labour force was so invested (Hinton, 1984), and in Vietnam, around 5–7% of labour time was so employed (Ministry of Agriculture, 1986).

The enhancement in both farm incomes and production in all three countries provided a large and growing domestic market for industry. Whilst this stimulated industrial growth in the national economy, it had a particularly positive effect on rural industry and what are termed 'sideline activities', which may include everything from bee-keeping to tailoring. What exports did for industrial growth in South Korea, the growth of the rural market did for North Korea, and particularly for China. The institution of the collective farm, expanded into the commune, was particularly suitable for both absorbing surplus labour, relating it to the available natural resources and capital within the particular area, and adjusting technologies to ensure utilization of local resources. The fact that a protected captive local market, within the framework of the command economy, could absorb the low-technology/low quality cement, fertilizer, bricks and metal products kept this programme of rural industrialization one of the most dynamic components of the economy (Sobhan, 1987). By 1978 in China, 9.3% of the rural labour force was employed in rural industry, a growth of 30% per year in the previous decade. By 1985, the share of the rural labour force in rural industry had doubled to 18.6%. This rapid growth of rural industry had raised its share of rural output to 42.3% by 1985. Today, in many areas of China, most households have become part-time farmers with the largest part of their income coming from non-agricultural activities.

Similarly in Vietnam, work-days invested by farm households in non-farm activities increased from 5.4% in 1960 to 18.2% in 1984 (Ministry of Agriculture, 1986). The increase in capital construction and non-farm activities has at the margin accounted for 50% of the increase in the average number of work-days invested by a household from 182 in 1960 to 292 in 1984.

The Cuban experience was somewhat different from that of the Asian economies in that the capitalist mode of production had already come to dominate the export-oriented agricultural economy. As we have seen, agrarian reform largely substituted the state for private capital as the owner of the land. The need for more intensive utilization of land was less apparent given Cuban factor proportions. Indeed, Cuba was one of the developing countries to experience an absolute contraction in its agricultural labour force from 813,000 in 1958–59 to 716,000 in 1979 (Brundenius, 1984). The proportion of agriculture in the labour force fell from 37% to 22% in this same period. This reflected in part the structural change in the Cuban economy whereby the share of agriculture declined from 18% in 1961 to 13% in 1981. Significant change took place within agriculture, however, with the mechanization of the sugar industry, which reduced the number of cane-cutters at peak harvest-time from 370,000 in 1957–58 to 100,000 in 1980–81 by increasing the mechanization of cutting from nil to 50% and load-lifting from nil to 100% over the same period. This released labour which was partially absorbed in other agricultural activities, but mostly outside agriculture, in industry and construction, where the labour force increased from 461,300 to 908,400 between 1958–59 and 1979 and its proportion in the labour force from 21 to 28%. Thus agrarian reform in Cuba was not a vehicle for more intensive utilization of rural labour, as in Asia, but for the structural diversification and technological upgrading of the Cuban economy.

The growth of agriculture and enhancement of factor productivity thus varied between the labour-surplus and labour-scarce socialist economies. In China, for example, there is some suggestion that factor productivity deteriorated from 100 to 91.5 in the first eight years of reform (Chao, 1972). Increase in output became a function of increased use of inputs in the way of labour, capital, including intermediate inputs. Agrarian reform thus becomes a vehicle for the diversion of resources into agriculture, and not necessarily an instrument for the more efficient use of resources. Where such resources are in fact derived from better utilization of underused capacities and the transfer of resources from unproductive sectors and superfluous consumption, this may be accepted as an appropriate trade-off for a decline in efficiency of factor use. To the extent that such resources need not necessarily have been used at all, or were being used less efficiently elsewhere in the economy, application of production function analysis may not be strictly relevant as a measure of the economic impact of agrarian reform.

The Ethiopian exception

The one exception to the general pattern of production increases, improved productivity and fuller employment associated with countries effecting a radical land reform is Ethiopia. This exception stems from the fact that in recent years crop failures, originating in severe drought conditions, and resulting in the publicized spectre of famine, continue to haunt the countryside. This picture is consistent with the evidence that agricultural production in Ethiopia grew at the rate of 2.1% between 1965 and 1973 and 1.2% between 1973 and 1984. Food production per capita remained static between 1974–76 and 1982–84 (World Bank, 1986, Table 6). The two time periods roughly coincide with the pre- and post-land reform periods, and indeed do not take account of the sharp decline in output associated with the famine of 1985 when agricultural production fell by an estimated 23% between 1984 and 1985 (World Bank, 1986 and 1987, Table 6). Since this failure of production has coincided with one of the most radical agrarian reforms, the temptation to equate failures of production with institutional change is strong although the impact of ongoing civil war cannot be ignored.

Available evidence does not, however, point to any noticeable deterioration in the treatment of agriculture in terms of public policy in Ethiopia after the revolution and agrarian reforms. Agriculture had been neglected by the *ancien régime* which may perhaps explain its sluggish performance even prior to 1974. Between 1969 and 1974, the years preceding the revolution, 6.1% of public expenditure went on agriculture. This in fact rose to 9.4% between 1975 and 1979, just after the revolution, and stabilized at 9% in the period 1980–84 (Sobhan, 1986). By the standards of other developing countries this was not a bad performance. This rise in the share of agriculture reflected a steady increase in the real value of public expenditure on agriculture between 1969–74 and 1983–84 when annual expenditure per capita of agricultural population in the recent period was four and a half times higher (Sobhan, 1986). One manifestation of improved public support was the increase in fertilizer use which rose from 0.4 kilograms per hectare in 1970 to 3.5 kilograms in 1984 (World Bank, 1987, Table 6).

In terms of public pricing policy, however, Ethiopia had pursued one of the most discriminatory policies in the developing world against its cereal producers. This pre-reform policy persisted after the revolution so that prices in real terms paid to cereal producers in 1981–83 were 45% below those in 1969–71 (FAO, 1985). This was the most severe price deterioration in 38 developing countries throughout the world. Furthermore the terms of trade against cereal producers in terms of fertilizer price deteriorated from an index of 100 in 1969–71 to 161 in 1981–83 (FAO, 1985).

Thus gains in public expenditure and input use in agriculture were not matched by adequate incentives to Ethiopia's farmers. It is, however, debatable whether improved price incentives could have made a decisive impact in the absence of much higher levels of investment in agriculture whereby supply could respond to market signals. Nor could it be argued that collectivization severely affected the farmer's commitment to produce, since by 1987 a maximum of 1.5% of the total agricultural area was cultivated in collective farms. Indeed, it might be argued that the minifundist holdings created by the reforms could not generate sufficient resources to effect modernization and yield increases. Some move towards stepping up the pace of collective production, which could reap economies of scale from larger public investment in agriculture, could in fact be an appropriate move to help a backward, disorganized and demoralized peasantry. This would, however, require an increase in public expenditure on agriculture which seems well beyond the means of what is one of the poorest countries in the world. Attempts to assist agriculture through Official Development Assistance (ODA) have been modest so that real per capita ODA to the agricultural sector in Ethiopia only increased from US$2.35 in 1974–79 to $4.14 in 1983–84 (Sobhan, 1986), and this was still one of the lowest levels of aid to agriculture in the developing world.

The severe ecological constraints to stimulating production, the ongoing civil wars (continuing even since the fall of the Mengistu regime) which inhibit sustained development activity and the paucity of investments in agriculture thus promise to keep agriculture in Ethiopia vulnerable to famines and unable to reap the potential benefits of agrarian reform.

THE ECONOMIC IMPACT OF AGRARIAN REFORM IN NON-EGALITARIAN ECONOMIES

Farm management performance

Outside those countries which have transformed relations of production and incorporated the entire peasantry within the compass of the reform, it is much more difficult to trace a direct link between reform and the overall direction of the agricultural economy. Only a few countries in Latin America, such as Mexico and Bolivia, and Egypt and Algeria in the Middle East, have involved a large enough proportion of land and households to make the reform itself into a possible variable influencing agricultural performance. The link between agrarian reform and agricultural economic performance could manifest itself in these economies because of abrupt changes in the operational control over the land. This may happen where traditional *haciendas* under the direct control of the *hacendado*, or plantations/capitalist farms run by owner-managers, are transferred to the ownership and control of household farms or transformed into state or collective or co-operative farms. This model of transition pertained in Mexico where *hacienda* lands were expropriated and placed within the *ejido* for distribution to individual households. Similarly in Bolivia *hacienda* lands seized after the 1952 revolution were parcelled out into family-sized holdings. It also applied to Peru where traditional *haciendas* in the highlands were incorporated into special producers' co-operatives where part of the land was cultivated jointly and part in small family holdings. In all three cases not only were former workers on the *haciendas* vested with control over the land but peasants in adjacent villages, quite unconnected with the land except through tenuous historical claims, were also given rights to this land (World Bank, 1978).

In contrast agrarian reforms which expropriated capitalist estates, as in the case of the sugar-cane plantations in the coastal areas of Peru, or in Chile, Nicaragua and the larger settler farms in Mozambique, Angola and Algeria or the tea plantations in Sri Lanka, the transition in operative control went from a modern private corporate entrepreneur to a collective of the former workers of the expropriated unit under the direction of state-appointed managers and technical support personnel. Cuba was the most extreme example of this transformation, and this has been discussed elsewhere. The post-colonial reforms in Zimbabwe and Kenya fall somewhere in between the two in that large settler estates, in all or part, were peacefully taken over by the state and distributed in individual holdings to new settlers who were sometimes former workers on the estate and sometimes farmers with no previous connection with the land in question. Whilst the Zimbabwean and much of the Kenyan model resembles much more closely the experience of Mexico and Bolivia, except that the process was peaceful and managed by the state, part of the Kenyan reforms sought to create capitalist farms, albeit on a smaller scale than the white settler farms. In recent years an emergent Kenyan bourgeoisie has been taking over intact entire estates hitherto owned by white settlers (Hunt, 1984). Here the mode of production remains unchanged and only the ethnic origin of the owner is changed.

Reforms involving a complete transformation in the management of the farm holdings as indicated above may be compared with reforms where ownership is transferred from a class of absentee owners to their former tenants who had all along been working the land. Agrarian reforms in Egypt, Iraq, Syria, the first-generation reforms evicting the superior tenure holders in India and Bangladesh, and the Marcos' land-to-the-tiller reforms in the Philippines all fall within this category. Here management of the operational unit is unchanged and only the terms on which land is cultivated and the incentive regime for cultivating the land have changed. It follows that in this last mentioned category of reforms the transition in the production regime will be much less severe than under reforms where management of the land changes completely.

The main point of departure between all such reforms and the reforms involving a complete redistribution of land lies in the fact that these reforms are only partial in their coverage. Thus elements of the *ancien régime*, whether as share-cropping landlords, as in India, Pakistan and Bangladesh and the Philippines, or large *hacendados* or capitalists, as in Mexico, Bolivia, Chile, Nicaragua, all of Central America, Pakistan, India, Egypt, Syria, Iraq, Tunisia,

Kenya and the Philippines, co-exist with the land reform beneficiaries. Indeed it is this class of share-cropping landowners and capitalist farmers who are the newly dominant elite in the post-reform agrarian system in inegalitarian agrarian societies. This class remains best equipped to benefit from state policies and investments designed to support the agricultural sector. Thus the direct benefits from the reform, which were clearly manifest in the socialist and the East Asian states due to the comprehensive access to state support, tend to become much more attenuated in the inegalitarian systems. The impact of the reform in such societies is registered through the possible transformation in the character of the former *hacendado*/landlord from an absentee or traditional owner interested only in expropriating the surplus into a modernizing capitalist farmer, using capital-intensive techniques on a smaller post-reform holding, shorn of surplus uncultivable lands. This model is visible in post-reform Mexico, Bolivia, Chile, India, Pakistan and Thailand. An agrarian system in which the dominant class has been transformed from a tradition-bound, inefficient and surplus-extracting feudal lord into a modern capitalist farmer may, however, be expected to be more productive if no less equitable or beneficial to the peasants.

Where share-croppers become owners, as in the rice lands of the Philippines or in Egypt, or where *colonatos*, estate workers or non-landowning peasants become direct owners of land, as in Mexico, Peru and Bolivia, there may be some stimulus, through their incentive to work the land more intensively, on land productivity. Where this land was hitherto uncultivated or under-cultivated, as in most of Latin America, placing poor peasants on such land is likely to be conducive to higher production. The hypothesis that a transition from the feudal to a capitalist or capitalist-cum-peasant mode will stimulate agricultural production can, of course, never be satisfactorily tested given the number of variables which may influence performance in particular countries at particular moments of time.

Agricultural output

In practice it is rare for an agrarian reform actually to coincide with a decline in production for any length of time. Cases where this occurred in the immediate aftermath of the reform are few and far between. The most conspicuous examples of such a decline are Angola and Mozambique. These countries could in principle be designated as socialist, but the prevailing co-existence of large state farms, small subsistence holdings and tribal tenure makes the system a transitional rather than a categorically socialist one, so we have analysed them with those systems classified as inegalitarian.

In the case of Mozambique agricultural production fell by 16.5% between 1980 and 1985 and the index of food production per capita fell to 98 in 1983–85 (1979–81 = 100) (World Bank, 1987, Tables 2 and 6). In the case of Angola the index of per capita food production in 1985 was 102, although this may have been well below levels prevailing in the pre-independence period (World Bank, 1987,

Table 6). Nicaragua also registered a decline in its rate of growth of agricultural production from 3.3% per year in the pre-reform period between 1965 and 1980 to 1.4% in 1980–85. As a result per capita food production in Nicaragua fell to 90 in 1983–85 (1979–81 = 100).

In all three cases the decline in production coincided with agrarian reforms under which large reasonably efficient capitalist farms owned by Portuguese settlers in Africa and by the Somoza family in Nicaragua were taken over and converted into state farms. In the case of Angola and Mozambique the withdrawal of the Portuguese not only meant a withdrawal of top management but also of most intermediate-level skills, so that the enterprises faced discernible declines in their technical capabilities. No such depreciation was evident in Nicaragua, however, as there was no shortage of technical or managerial personnel to run the farms. The common feature of all three countries was the impact of a protracted and debilitating externally sponsored and sustained insurgency which diverted resources and disrupted production. It would therefore, at least in the case of Nicaragua, be unfair to equate the reform with the decline in production, and indeed there are many indicators of public policies and investments designed to improve the circumstances of the *campesinos* in Nicaragua (Peek, 1986).

The agrarian reforms in Bolivia may have had a temporarily disruptive effect due to the period of social dislocation arising from the violent upheaval which drove *Hacendados* from their estates and led to lands being forcibly occupied by *colonatos* and even outside villagers. However once the new order settled down, production of most major crops increased quite sharply between 1950 and 1972. The poor man's crop, potato, increased from 189,000 tons in 1950 to an annual 351,000 tons in the years 1957 to 1961 and to 643,000 tons in 1972 (World Bank, 1978). Similarly production of maize, rice and barley all registered noticeable increases. Even wheat, production of which fell initially, registered an increase from 46,000 tons in 1950 to 59,000 tons between 1968 and 1972 (World Bank, 1978). It is only in recent years, long after the impact of the reform had worked itself out, that the rate of growth of agricultural production has fallen from 3.5% between 1965–73 to 1.1% between 1973–84 (World Bank, 1986, Table 2). Food production per capita has thus fallen to 84 in 1982–84 (1974–76 = 100) (World Bank, 1986, Table 6).

The other two countries where the agrarian reform has coincided with a decline in the agricultural economy are Iraq and Syria. In the Iraqi case agricultural production stagnated in the post-reform period, 1965–73, at a growth rate of 1.7% a year (World Bank, 1986, Table 2), while in Syria production fell between 1965 and 1973 at an annual rate of 0.7%. The available evidence is insufficient to confirm that this decline coincided with agrarian reforms. In the case of Iraq, we have seen that much of the land was held by absentee owners but in the newly irrigated areas some of these landlords had been taking back control over land for capitalist agriculture. In the case of Syria the incidence of the reform did not really hit at the capitalist owners since, as in Iraq, retention limits were left high enough to leave potential or actual capitalist farmers undisturbed. Thus the decline in output must coincide less with the reform than the attendant policy regime and neglect of agriculture which coincided with the Iraqi reform. Abundant oil revenues certainly provided reasons to be less supportive of agriculture (Warriner, 1969), although in recent years there was some stimulus to food production so that the index rose in 1983–85 to 114 from a 1978–81 level of 100 (World Bank, 1987, Table 6). Despite this increase, Iraq had to increase its cereal imports from 870,000 tons in 1974 to 3.4 million in 1985 (World Bank, 1987).

In the case of Syria there has been an increase in agricultural production which rose by 6.4% between 1980 and 1985, and food production per capita was 108 in 1983–85 (1979–81 = 100) (World Bank, 1987); however cereal imports were up from 339,000 tons in 1974 to 1.1 million in 1985.

In the two other countries where major reforms took place, Chile and Peru, trends in agricultural production are mixed. In the Peruvian case the rate of growth of agriculture clearly fell in the wake of the reform from 2% in the period 1965–73 to 1.2% in the period 1973–84 (World Bank, 1987). Food production per capita, however, picked up in 1983–85 to an index of 111 (1979–81 = 100), though imports of cereals nearly doubled from 637,000 tons in 1974 to 1.2 million in 1985 (World Bank, 1987). In the case of Chile production appears to have declined in the years of the reform, 1965–73, by 1.1% per year but picked up to a 3.4% growth rate in the 1973–84 period. In recent years, however, growth may have been reversed and output fallen.

Agrarian reform and the improvement of agricultural production

In contrast to these episodes of negative or modest growth in the wake of agrarian reform, the two success stories in the non-radical reform countries have been Algeria and Mexico. Algeria faced a serious problem of filling the vacuum created by the departure of the *colons* after independence in 1962 and the consequent transition from capitalist agriculture to its system of *autogestion*. In the aftermath of the reform, output grew by an annual average of 2.4% between 1965 and 1973, and this picked up to 4.2% between 1973 and 1984 (World Bank, 1986). In this period, however, food production per capita increased to an index of 108 in 1983–85 (1979–81 = 100), but cereal imports also increased from 1.8 million tons in 1974 to 5.3 million tons, so the increase in production clearly lagged behind that in demand. Oil revenues appear to have reduced pressure to stimulate food production since they were sufficient to finance the food gap.

Algeria has not neglected its agricultural sector, but neither has it really managed to realize the potential which it had inherited and which liberal investment of oil revenues would have made realizable. Whilst Algeria may have lost the tied French markets which stimulated *colon* agriculture, its fast-growing domestic market fuelled by oil wealth could provide all the stimulus Algerian farmers need to sustain improvements in agriculture. An inability to satisfy local demand for cereals (40%), pulses (45%), milk and dairy products (40%) has not been compensated by full or almost complete self-sufficiency in meat, poultry products, fruit and vegetables (*South*, Dec. 1986), and agricultural imports remain a major drain on foreign exchange. Food imports account for 19% of merchandise imports. It remains debatable whether this moderate performance of the agricultural sector could have been improved by converting state farms to small individual holdings. Since the retention of capitalist farms was never a serious policy option, the present policy of reducing the state farms from their present size of 1,500–2,000 hectares to smaller, more economically manageable units of 100 hectares run by between three and seven producers will be more conducive to faster growth of output (*South*, Dec. 1986).

The other success story was, of course, Mexico. The extent of the reform which distributed 60 million hectares, 43% of all farm land, to nearly two million households, 66% of all agricultural households, made it a test case for the success of a non-socialist agrarian reform. The fact that agricultural output in Mexico grew by 4.6% a year between 1940 and 1960, just after the most extensive reforms carried through by President Cardenas, was seen as testimony to the impact of the reform (World Bank, 1978). In this period the growth rate in the rest of Latin America was 2.7%. Prior to this, agricultural growth in Mexico had been sluggish, and the fact that this growth coincided with the high tide of the small *ejido* farms, which accounted for 69% of all farms and 46% of the farm area in 1970, was seen as evidence of the success of a redistributive reform which transferred the lands of large *hacendados* to smallholders.

This period of growth coincided with the advent of the green revolution of which Mexico was the pioneer in the Third World. The government was also generally supportive of agriculture in its investment strategies, diverting its recources to bring large areas under irrigation.

Mexico's agricultural growth rates in these initial decades was sustained. Between 1965 and 1973 agricultural output grew at a rate of 5.4% a year, one of the highest rates in the Third World (World Bank, 1986, Table 2). In the subsequent 1973–84 period growth rates fell to 3.4%, but this was still impressive by the standards of other developing countries (World Bank, 1986). Food production per capita stood at 110 in 1983–85 (1979–81 = 100) (World Bank, 1987, Table 6). Nevertheless Mexico was actually importing 4.5 million tons of cereals in 1985 – substantially more than the 4.2 million in 1974, and these accounted for 17% of the country's total merchandise imports.

During the 1970s, Mexico's policy regime became somewhat less supportive of agriculture. Per capita public expenditure on agriculture, which had continued to increase until the mid-1970s, fell in the 1980–84 period. Whilst this may have reflected the impact of IMF-imposed austerity measures, the share of expenditure on agriculture declined sharply from 13% in 1969–74 to 4.8% in 1983–84 (Sobhan, 1986). This decline was faster than that of agriculture's share in GDP. Pricing policy, however, remained supportive of both cereals and export crops, particularly the latter, between 1969 and 1983, and the terms of trade moved in a generally favourable direction for Mexican agriculture (FAO, 1985). These trends were, however, not sufficient to sustain the dynamic of Mexican agriculture which had characterized its performance for more than three decades following the agrarian reform of the 1940s.

Inequitable growth: the Mexican experience

The success of Mexican agriculture already carried the seeds of dualism which have now contributed to the slow-down of growth and the emergence of a large landless proletariat three decades after Latin America's most radical reform outside Cuba. The spectacular growth of the 1950–70 period in Mexico was essentially confined to the larger producers, and a study of this growth shows that between 1950 and 1960, some 80% of the growth of output was accounted for by the most affluent farms which made up just 3.5% of all farming units (World Bank, 1978). Indeed during this period the poorest farms, 50% of the total, experienced a decline in production; these poorer farms accounted for 4% of total output, compared to 54% contributed by the top 3.5%.

Even within the *ejidos* some element of dualism had begun to manifest itself. The top 2% of *ejido* farms, with mean annual outputs of $2,000 and above, recorded an average output of $3,500, compared with $45 for the 46% of farms at the lowest end of the scale and $270 for the next 38% in the production scale. The cultivated area was six times higher between the top 2% of the *ejido* farms and the bottom 46%, and the value of machinery used was 150 times higher. Where the irrigated area was 94% for the most affluent units, it was nil for 82% of all farms. Thus yields in the richest farms were 129 times higher than for the poorest farms. In 1970, 74% of maize output in *ejidos* was contributed by the top 22% of farms whilst the poorest 78% accounted for 26% of output. If one notes that in 1950 the contribution of the poorest farms accounted for 48% of output compared to 52% in the most affluent *ejido* farms, the trend becomes apparent.

It is, therefore, hardly surprising that the number of rural landless families in Mexico, which had fallen from 1.1 million in 1910 to 200,000 in 1940, had risen again by 1960 to 1.28 million, some 35% of all farm families (World Bank, 1978). If we add the landless and minifundists together they represented 48% of all farm households in 1960, and this class of landless and land-poor had by the 1970s risen to 60% (Sinha, 1984). It was only appropriate that a micro study in Mexico should show that 71% of farm households, with holdings below four hectares, should derive 58% of their annual income from selling their labour for wages and depend on farm production for only 32% of their income (de Janvry, 1981). The fact that 49% of rural households in Mexico should in 1970 be classified as being below the poverty line produces an appropriate measure of the fate of a radical land reform which retained differentiation in the access to land (World Bank, 1978).

The fate of Mexican agrarian reform is, of course, mirrored in all those countries which have legislated reforms, with or without effecting a transition in relations of production, which have left a basis for differentiation within the peasantry and for the market mechanism to accentuate this differentiation.

The persistence of rural differentiation

Table 1 shows that in all countries other than the seven which underwent radical reform, landlessness has persisted in the post-reform phase; access to land remains inequitable; a rising proportion of the rural population in these countries depends on selling its labour rather than on cultivation of land for its principal source of livelihood and the proportion of rural households classified as living in conditions of poverty remains high. This tendency may be moderated in particular countries by the relative strength of the economy, but nonetheless remains fairly widespread amongst the countries discussed by us in Chapter 5. Table 1 measures these manifestations of rural backwardness, and we can see that the proportion of the landless and land-poor was 85% in Bolivia, 75% in Peru and 53% in Chile (1973). In Egypt it stood at 29% for totally landless but in 1965, even after the reform, 94.5% of the farm households were still cultivating only 57% of the land, in holdings of less than five acres, which on average came to 1.26 acres per household; little wonder a high proportion of these households were selling their labour on the market to ensure subsistence (King, 1977).

We have observed that landless and minifundist households which have to sell their labour have persisted even in those societies that have effected a sizeable redistribution of land sufficient to ensure some form of transition in the relations of production. It is thus more than likely that in South and South-East Asia, in Central America, in Kenya and Tunisia, where the compass of agrarian reforms was limited and the commitment to social transformation much weaker, agrarian reforms would have made little impact on the large and growing segment of the rural population which remains landless or has insufficient land to ensure subsistence. These countries in most cases kept ceilings so high that there was not enough land taken over by the state to provide adequately for all landless households or sufficiently to augment all minifundist land holdings so as to take them above the minimum holding needed for subsistence. Furthermore, high retention limits enabled a large degree of differentiation to prevail within the peasantry so that a dominant class continued to survive in the rural areas. These dominant classes included ex-landowners share-cropping land in South and South-East Asia; reconstituted landowners in varying degrees of transition to capitalist farming in Latin America, the Middle East, India, Pakistan and Thailand; rich peasant capitalists in all of South and South-East Asia, Egypt, Kenya, Tunisia; corporate farms left untouched by agrarian reforms in much of Latin America, in tea plantations in India, Bangladesh and Sri Lanka (until nationalization); and corporate, in many cases foreign-controlled, plantations in Thailand, Indonesia and the Philippines.

These differentiations were manifest in the high gini-coefficients for land-ownership registered in Table 1. Here again the degrees of inequality in Latin America remain much more extreme than in Asia, Africa and even the Middle East. Even where massive redistributions of land took place, the gini-coefficient remains high. Thus in Mexico the gini-coefficient in 1970 stood as high as 0.938, higher than Brazil (0.837) which went through no discernible agrarian reform. In 1970 in Bolivia, 1% of households still controlled 65% of the land whilst 51% operated holdings of over 1,000 hectares (World Bank, 1978). In Peru, less than 0.1% of households still controlled 35% of the land in holdings above 1,000 hectares whilst 59% of households, untouched by the reform, held 6% of the land, (World Bank, 1978). In Chile, 6% of households with holdings above 20 hectares still held 42% of the land after the completion of the Allende reform of 1972 whilst 66% of the households held 10% of the land (World Bank, 1978).

Whilst inequalities in access to land persist even where reforms have taken place, control over land in most parts of the world exposed to agrarian reform has resulted in less severe differentiation than in Latin America. Despite this, inequality remains considerable. Thus in Kenya, in 1981, the gini-coefficient stood at 0.77 despite the extensive redistribution of settler lands; the concentration index is a good measure of the differentiation created by the birth of an indigenous capitalist class in Kenya. In the Philippines, the gini-coefficient for land holdings in 1981, well after the Marcos reforms, stood at 0.53, a deterioration compared to the index of 0.51 in 1971 on the eve of the reforms. In Algeria, despite the socialist intent of its agrarian reforms, the gini-coefficient still stood at 0.72 in 1973.

In South Asia holdings also remain unequal. In India land holdings actually became more concentrated between 1960 (0.61) and 1977 (0.62). In Sri Lanka after the 1970 agrarian reforms, the gini-coefficient actually stood at 0.62 compared to 0.51 in 1973, but in Sri Lanka, as in Algeria, this may reflect the fact that nationalized plantations are still held in large operational units. Bangladesh and Pakistan have relatively more equitable patterns of ownership. In Pakistan this reflects the impact of two agrarian reforms in the 1960s and 1970s as a result of which the gini-coefficient came down from 0.61 in 1960 to 0.54 in 1980, but in Bangladesh a less egalitarian pattern of holdings registered a gini-coefficient of 0.60 in 1983–84, and more recent evidence suggests that this may have deteriorated (Rahman et al., 1987). The index further conceals the fact that many large holdings in Bangladesh have been nominally redistributed to escape ceiling legislation under the agrarian reforms of 1972, which set the land ceiling at 33 acres, and also to evade land tax which at that period exempted holdings below eight acres.

The different impact of radical and non-egalitarian reforms on rural differentiation

The persistence of landlessness and minifundist holdings in the post-reform phase and the prevalence of inequalities in access to land throughout these countries which have experienced various measures of agrarian reform over the last four decades established the critical difference between the egalitarian reforms of the socialist and East Asian countries and the reforms enacted by all other countries discussed here. The 'radical' reformers totally eliminated the once dominant class as a social and economic force in the countryside. By setting and enforcing sufficiently low ceilings, the radical reforms pre-empted the emergence of a new dominant class. By ensuring uniform access to public resources and services for all farm households, whether in the collectivist mode of the socialist system or the peasant mode of East Asia, they ensured that agricultural growth, improvements in levels of living and accumulation whether at low or high levels would be shared amongst all land reform beneficiaries. In contrast, the inegalitarian agrarian reforms, operating within a market system and exposed to demographic pressures, ensured that inequalities would persist. The emergence of a dominant class ensured that access to scarce public resources would be inequitably distributed to the dominant groups. This accentuated dualism by which the rich farmers would prosper and the poverty of the landless/land-poor would be perpetuated. This process, compounded by demographic pressures, would lead to loss of land so that the number of the land-poor and landless would increase and the class of wage-earners seeking to sell their labour to capitalist farms and in non-agricultural employment would grow. These developments in the post-reform phase would thus frustrate the original logic of the land reform to provide equitable access to agricultural land.

The disenchantment with agrarian reforms since the 1970s reflects the failure of agrarian reform in most countries to bring about more equitable access to land. Whilst much emphasis is placed on weakness of implementation, particularly in South Asia (Herring, 1985), our study argues that the real problem lies in the weakness of conception. The land redistributions effected by the reforms in Mexico, Bolivia, Peru, Chile, Egypt, Syria and Iraq were not insignificant by any standards. Indeed, the Mexican and Bolivian reforms touched a higher proportion of farm households than the reforms in South Korea. The real problem lies in the fact that the reforms could not eliminate differentiation in the countryside and this failure in turn reflected the correlation of class forces behind the reforms. The mobilizations by coalitions of the middle class and peasants in Latin America, or the top-down reforms by middle-class reformers in the Middle East, South and South-East Asia and Africa, could not take land away from owners beyond the upper layers of the landed elite, and in many cases could not even touch them, as was the case in Central America and Pakistan. The more ubiquitous rich peasant/kulak/bullock-capitalist strata and the reconstituted landlord/*hacendado* thus become part of the new ruling coalitions of these countries, with roots in the countryside, unlike the absentee landowners of the *ancien régime*. The links forged with a stronger and more resourceful state by this new rural elite have vested it with more pervasive and durable instruments of control outside the land, in the form of dominance in factor markets for capital, inputs and indeed for absorption of labour in the capitalist sector. Even share-cropping, where it persisted, has been incorporated into a pattern of market relations which has penetrated traditional agriculture in the wake of the green revolution.

7. The Rationale for Agrarian Reform Today

It is self-evident that outside those countries which have carried through radical agrarian reforms, the circumstances which created the need for agrarian reform are no less pressing today than they were in the past. We may attempt to identify some of these pressures in terms of the social conditions from which the need for reform originates. In some countries these reforms were so conceived that the reasons which may have been moderated by an earlier generation of reforms have now resurfaced. In other countries agrarian reforms were so inadequate both in their conception and their extent that the original pressures have merely been reinforced by the passage of time. In only a very few countries has the need to initiate new reforms been eradicated either by the success of the old reforms or the development of alternatives to such reforms which have removed the need for further reform. When we review the need for further reforms we will, therefore, review some of the alternatives to agrarian reform which have, with varying degress of efficacy, been attempted by governments disinclined and/or constrained to pursue agrarian reforms. Given the wide geo-political and historical canvas covered by such a review, we will limit our discussion here to an impressionistic survey of the problem in the light of our earlier discussion of different national experiences of reform and its impact.

Trends in rural landlessness

As we have already observed, one of the most potent forces generating pressure for agrarian reform lay in the lack of access to lands for a high proportion of the agricultural population. The evidence cited in Chapter 4 and encapsulated in Table 2 suggests that landlessness is still a major problem in most countries which have effected agrarian reforms and, *a fortiori*, in those which have effected only weak or negligible reforms. If we use the concept of landlessness to include those land-poor households without enough land to ensure their subsistence, then we should include both such groups in our assessment of the need for agrarian reform. We have already seen that, in countries which have implemented reforms, landlessness remains high in Mexico (60%), Bolivia (85%), Peru (75%), Chile (53%), Egypt (60%), Kenya (32%), India (55%), Bangladesh (78%), Pakistan (34%), Sri Lanka (43%), the Philippines (60%)

and Indonesia (71%). This list, of course, includes a number of countries which went in for reform, and those such as Brazil which did not have a large segment of their rural population in desperate need of land.

Rural Poverty

The persistence of landlessness in rural areas long after the reform indicates not just the inadequacy of the reforms but also that alternatives to land reform have not developed to the point where pressure for land has been eased. In such countries rural poverty also persists in the form of hunger and malnutrition, and Table 2 shows levels of poverty and landlessness. It shows that, where the evidence exists, the persistence of poverty does indeed correlate with the unsatisfied land-hunger of the rural population. In Brazil (73%), Costa Rica (34%), Honduras (80%), Nicaragua (80%), El Salvador (76%), Guatemala (84%), Peru (68%), Mexico (49%), Syria (54%), Egypt, India, Bangladesh, Sri Lanka, the Philippines and Indonesia, rural poverty is seen as the end-product of the inability to ensure sufficient access to land in order to make possible an adequate livelihood.

Demographic pressures

This failure of agrarian reform to release enough land to the growing numbers of the landless is again, within the prevailing distribution of land, a measure of demographic pressures. These pressures relate the expansion in the cultivable area to changes in agricultural population and labour force. Whilst population growth is ubiquitous, if varying in its intensity, in the developing world, the expansion of acreage of arable land to absorb this growth is restricted to countries which can bring unused land under cultivation through land distribution and/or investment in land development. It must be borne in mind that failure to extend the cultivable area can be compensated for by raising the productivity through investment in irrigation, technology improvements and mechanization. A deterioration in the availability of land must therefore be evaluated in the context of the specific circumstances governing investment in the agricultural sector before drawing any conclusion about the contribution of demographic pressures to land poverty.

Table 3 shows that amongst countries evaluated by us, mostly in South America but also in parts of South-East Asia, land availability for cultivation per agricultural household increased between 1969 and 1984 (Sobhan, 1986). In Latin America this includes Bolivia, Chile, Colombia, Costa Rica, Cuba, Peru, Venezuela and non-reform Brazil. In South-East Asia, however, Indonesia, Thailand and even the Philippines improved their land/labour ratios, as did Tunisia. However throughout most of Central America, South Asia, the Middle East and Africa, and even in South Korea and Taiwan, the ratio of land per capita of agricultural labour force deteriorated. Investment in raising the yield of the land in Taiwan and South Korea, in contrast to investment in land development in such countries as Brazil and Indonesia, ensured that the average circumstances of peasant households in the former group of land-scarce countries is, if anything, better than the latter, more land-abundant countries.

However amongst countries facing a deterioration in their population–land ratio, the following tried to counteract this tendency by expanding their area of irrigated land and/or the area on which fertilizer was used: Algeria (both), Bangladesh (both), Taiwan (both), Egypt (fertilizer only), Ecuador (both), El Salvador (irrigation only), Ethiopia (both), Guatemala (both), Honduras (both), Iraq (both), Kenya (both), South Korea (both), Mexico (both), Mozambique (irrigation only), Nicaragua (both), Pakistan (both), Panama (both), Sri Lanka (both), Syria (both) and Zimbabwe (both) (Sobhan, 1986).

Thus demographic pressures do indeed constitute a pressure on land, but this is not insoluble given the potential for increasing the carrying capacity of the land. Demographic pressure is really exercised at the lower end of the scale, so a 3% growth in population on a 20-hectare farm can be compensated for by yield-enhancing investments, but similar pressure on a two-hectare farm can force the household into debt, sale of land and refuge in the labour market. This explains why countries in Latin America which have brought new land under cultivation still have to live with rising numbers of the landless or land-poor in their rural areas. The expansion of the arable area in such countries may well be taken advantage of by capitalist farmers, who may indeed have contributed to this expansion by bringing more of their own uncultivated land into cultivation.

Rural under-employment

Demographic pressures put limits on the capacity of the land. This leads to growth of under-employment of the agricultural labour force. Apart from the radical agrarian reformers, other countries studied by us still sustain high rates of under-employment in the rural economy along with high levels of landlessness, even after enacting agrarian reforms. Table 3 indicates levels of under-employment in a number of developing countries which have experienced agrarian reforms. Thus in Chile under-employment in agriculture increased from 11% on the eve of the reform to 21% in 1977, and was still 17% in 1980; total unemployment in 1983 was estimated at 34%. Peru, despite a major agrarian reform, had an estimated under-employment figure of 61% in 1982 for its agricultural labour force. El Salvador reported under-employment of 47% in agriculture in 1975 and open unemployment of 27% in 1980. Brazil registered an under-employment rate in agriculture of 29.2% in 1980 (de Janvry et al., 1986).

Under-employment has also been a characteristic feature of the agricultural economy in most of South and South-East Asia, and indeed Africa. We will not try to detail the evidence here. Outside South Korea, and Taiwan, labour absorption outside agriculture has not been sufficient to reduce levels of under-employment and landlessness in Asia.

Table 3
Land Availability, Rural Underemployment and Real Wages

	(1) Index of Land Availability, 1980–84 (1969 = 100) (Arable Land Per Capita for Agricultural Labour Force)	(2) % of Rural Underemployment	(3) Growth Trends in Agricultural Real Wages (1965–84)		
			1965–74	1974–80	1980–84
1. Bolivia	131.5				
2. Chile	119.7	11 (1970) 17 (1980)	+2.7	+4.7	–12.2
3. Mexico	96.9		+3.7	+1.0	–15.0
4. Peru	112.0	68 (1975) 61 (1982)			
5. Nicaragua	88.6				
6. Costa Rica	102.3		+4.2	+11.7	–4.5
7. Honduras	80.4				
8. El Salvador	85.6	89 (1965) 47 (1975)			
9. Guatemala	91.9		–11.7	–3.4	+3.1
10. Panama	95.7		+3.6	+1.3	–3.3
11. Venezuela	101.8				
12. Ethiopia	88.3		1969/74 +	1975/79 +	1980–84
13. Kenya	76.4		10.4	14.3	
14. Zimbabwe	88.4		+14.2	+50.5	

15.	Mozambique	85.4		
16.	Angola	81.1		
17.	Algeria	97.5		
18.	Tunisia	104.6		
19.	Egypt	68.4		
20.	Iraq	85.8		
21.	Syria	67.3		
22.	Pakistan	86.4		
23.	India	91.7	40 (1980)	
24.	Bangladesh	70.2		−13.2
25.	Sri Lanka	85.1		−17.1
26.	Indonesia	104.5		
27.	Philippines	109.2		
28.	Thailand	117.8		
29.	South Korea	97.6	+57.6	+40.2
30.	China (Taiwan)	92.5		
31.	Cuba	175.2		

Sources:

1. Sobhan, 1986.
2. Latin America: de Janvry, 1986.
   Bangladesh: Hirashima and Muqtada, 1986.
3. Sobhan, 1986.

Rural wage trends

The high levels of under-employment and landlessness in most developing countries is manifest in the stagnation of real wages in the rural economy. Table 3 shows that between 1971 and 1984 in Africa, real wages in agriculture declined for seven out of a sample of nine countries (ILO, 1987). Of those countries which have experienced land reform, real wages in 1984 stood at an index of 87 compared to 113 in Kenya in 1971, while in Zimbabwe real wages rose to 164 in 1983 compared to 86 in 1971.

In Asia, real wages in agriculture also tended to stagnate or decline between 1969 and 1984 in India, Bangladesh, Sri Lanka and the Philippines (ILO, 1987). Only in South Korea and Pakistan did real wages rise during this period (Sobhan, 1986). Similarly in Latin America, amongst countries which undertook agrarian reform, real wages in agriculture fell in Chile, Ecuador and Mexico, but rose in Colombia and Panama, except between 1980 and 1984 when they also fell there. In countries which have not experienced reform, wages fell in Brazil, Guatemala, Paraguay, Uruguay and Argentina. The only country to register a rise was Costa Rica, where wages rose 11.7% between 1974 and 1979, but fell by 4.5% from 1979 to 1983 (ILO, 1987).

Trends in the fall in real wages are thus consistent with trends in under-employment in agriculture and the persistence of rural poverty, demonstrating that alternatives both within and outside agriculture have not grown fast enough, and that urban areas have become breeding grounds for under-employment, poverty and declining real wages.

New technology in agriculture

The development of the new high-yielding varieties of seeds associated with the green revolution suggested for a while that hope for increased labour absorption in agriculture lay in the diffusion of new technology. This process, it was believed, could arrest the fall in real wages and the growth in under-employment and rural poverty. Despite the high rates of growth in agricultural production associated with the green revolution, its full benefits have not been able to percolate through to the rural poor on a sufficient scale to arrest the growth of rural poverty.

The distributive failures of the green revolution have been more manifest in Latin America, where the green revolution has inequitably benefited rich farmers who could command the capital resources necessary to make the best use of the new technology (Griffin, 1974). The tendency for the *hacendado/* capitalist farmers of Latin America to choose more capital-intensive technologies and land-intensive cropping patterns has meant that abundant labour has been absorbed at a much slower rate than might have been expected during a period of rising production (de Janvry, 1981).

In the agricultural economies of Monsoon Asia, however, the techniques associated with high-yielding varieties have been more efficient in absorbing surplus labour. The scale-neutral nature of the technology has meant that its adoption has usually stimulated the use of both household and hired labour (Hirashima and Muqtada, 1986). Nor has the new technology bypassed small farmers, who have indeed become even more efficient adapters than the rich farmers, largely because small farms have the requisite surplus labour per unit of land to invest in the adoption of the potentially labour-intensive technology (Hossain, 1987). The Asian peasants' need to use high-yielding varieties where they can is due to desperate poverty, and they have turned to yield-enhancing technology to sustain the declining capacity of the land to feed growing families.

The rapid spread of the new technology throughout Asia has, however, only marginally reduced the rate of growth of rural poverty. It has neither reduced rates of poverty nor reversed its growth except in the countries which have carried through radical agrarian reforms. Given the need for circulating capital to sustain technology adaptation, even for the smallest farmers, inequitable access to the capital market has meant that technological diffusion, within the prevailing social order, has been much slower than it might have been in a more equitable social system. Indeed, given the fact that the richer farmers have, if anything, been less efficient users of high-yielding varieties, a more equitable downward redistribution of land would, at least in Monsoon Asia, have ensured a more rapid adoption of new technology and the expansion of productive forces.

The spread of new technologies has been much less pronounced in the Middle East and Africa. In these two regions capitalist agriculture, and even the large state farms of Algeria, have been more capital-intensive in their choice of technologies than is justified by the availability of under-employed labour in their respective countries. This labour surplus is perhaps less true of the Middle East where, except for Egypt and Algeria, which exports labour to France, labour was much more of a constraint to development given the distortions introduced by the abundant oil revenues of the region. In Africa, however, there is no doubt that labour absorption, and consequently land utilization, would have been greatly facilitated by a more equitable distribution of land.

The scope for labour absorption outside agriculture

The limits of technological diffusion adequately to enhance the carrying capacity of agricultural land can, of course, be compensated for by diversification of employment opportunities both within the rural economy and in the national economy. To the extent that labour absorption outside agriculture can keep pace with, or even outstrip, the growth in rural population, the growth of landlessness and rural poverty can be contained and real rural wages increase.

We have already observed that, in the case of the radical agrarian reformers of East Asia, demographic pressures on post-reform agricultural lands were contained by the rapid export-led industrialization of the economy. Agrarian reform has the virtue that at the initial stage, by distributing land to a large segment of the rural population, it contributes to a reduction in the numbers of the rural poor competing for work, so the immediate pressure on the industrial sector to mop up the surplus can be initially reduced.

This surplus rural labour entering the job market is, however, not drawn just from landless households but also from small farm households with surplus labour. An increase in family size in such landowning households need not lead to further land fragmentation and the growth of minifundism if the additional labour can be absorbed outside agriculture. The regression which took place in Mexico, where land reform beneficiaries in the two decades after the reform were forced to sell off their lands and once again swell the ranks of the landless, did not take place in South Korea or Taiwan because of the pervasiveness of their agrarian reform and the pace of industrial development in those countries.

The Asian socialist model of labour absorption was slightly different to that of the East Asian approach insofar as programmes for absorbing surplus household labour were built into the collectivization process. It is arguable that whilst collectivization in the USSR was dictated by the need for the state to monopolize the grain surplus, in the Asian socialist economies it was an institutional device to ensure full employment of surplus labour. This surplus labour was seen as being insufficiently absorbed through the market mechanism due to the 'stickiness' of wages. The only scope lies in the self-exploitation of such labour within the household, usually for low-rewarding or low-productivity tasks, and even this is constrained by lack of access to land or capital; this surplus labour nevertheless co-exists with an under-developed rural infrastructure and community services.

Neither the market nor the fiscal mechanism can mobilize savings to marry the under-employed labour with the need for rural development. In many developing countries, foreign aid for various rural works programmes has become the mainstay for such exercises in labour absorption (Sobhan, 1968). Unfortunately, the use of foreign aid to build up the rural infrastructure removes pressure from the rural rich to raise their domestic savings or contributions to public revenue to pay wages to the landless to develop the rural infrastructure. Thus both labour absorption and rural development have in one developing country after another become dependent on foreign-aid programmes (Sobhan, 1983).

The Asian socialist model of collectivist development has become a most effective instrument for using such surplus labour for collective investments. The compensation for this labour comes not from wages but from enhanced productivity of the land as a result of the increased value of the land's produce due to improved rural roads and the rise in consumption of collective public services provided by newly developed services. This approach to compensation is only possible within a collectivist framework in which all households in the village have more or less equal access to the usufruct of the land.

Where land is inequitably owned, by contrast, the beneficiaries of a newly dug irrigation channel, terracing of new lands or construction of a dam will be the owners of land served by this investment. Those who work to develop such lands will thus only do so for wages. If the owners of land prefer to divert their financial surpluses outside agriculture for reasons of security or yield and/or wait for aid donors to finance the construction of new flood control and irrigation works, then idle labour will continue to remain idle.

In China, Vietnam and North Korea, by pooling labour within the collective, labour which was surplus to the needs of crop cultivation in a particular area could be deployed in infrastructure development, planting trees along rural roads, animal husbandry and many other activities which can enhance the domestic resource use and hence wealth of the rural community. There are undoubtedly some diseconomies in this separation of labour from its immediate fruits, but even the system of work points used in the collectives of socialist Asia do translate into some household claims on the collective wealth created by such investment of labour.

In contemporary China there is a tendency to move away from this collective deployment of labour to build the infrastructure and in parts of the country work is now being contracted out to groups of households, under the Household Responsibility System, to work exclusively on infrastructure projects, road maintenance or arboriculture. This has yet to prove itself, since it is by no means certain that the cash surplus of the community will ensure full employment of household labour or ensure a sufficient development of the rural infrastructure or its maintenance.

There is some indication that there has been a decline in such investments and a running down of collective facilities, which may erode the basis for future growth in land productivity. The rapid advances in agricultural productivity being registered in China today are no doubt due to the enhanced incentives provided to farmers under the new Household Responsibility System, but it is also arguable that the capacity to respond to these incentives has been immeasurably improved by the collective investments of labour in building the water-control systems and development of land which over the years took place under the aegis of the collective/commune framework (Hinton, 1984).

As we have observed in Chapter 3, the other feature of the socialist system, particularly in China, was to develop rural industry and side-line activities. This too becomes an effective vehicle for labour absorption, creating real demand to sustain agricultural growth and providing resources for autonomous rural development and enhanced household incomes and consumption. The Chinese model of labour absorption through rural development outside agriculture seems the answer for countries with labour surpluses seeking to both decentralize the benefits of development and to do so by a more autonomous process of balanced development which internalizes the spread effects of development within a rural community (Sobhan, 1987).

The socialist countries have, however, apart from high rates of labour absorption in the rural areas, also sustained rapid rates of industrialization, particularly in China and North Korea. Industry in China grew at an annual rate of 12.1% between 1965 and 1973, 8.7% between 1973 and 1984 and 11.1% between 1980 and 1985 (World Bank, 1987, Table 2). China raised the share of manufactures in its GDP from 30% in 1965 to 37% in 1985, which makes it the most industrialized country of the Third World with a sustained rate of growth in industry matched only by South Korea. Unlike South Korea, and indeed most industrializing countries in the Third World, rural industrialization has made an important contribution to this process in China.

We have seen the evidence that both North Korea and Cuba have also sustained high rates of industrialization and structural change, which has eased the pressure on the land. Evidence from Vietnam is less conclusive, and industry accounted for only 12% of its labour force in 1980, compared to 6% in 1965 (World Bank, 1987, Table 32). This may be a legacy from the long period of war which constrained development and diversification of the economy.

High rates of industrial growth within the socialist agrarian reform countries are again consistent with the traditional self-reliant model of economic growth pioneered by the USSR. Whilst questions may be raised about the efficiency of this pattern of growth, and the need to carry it to the extremes associated with this model, there is enough evidence to indicate that it has contributed to high rates of industrial growth. This has been possible because of the rapid growth of the domestic market in the wake of agrarian reforms and its impact on the democratization of purchasing power.

However the East Asian radical reformers, South Korea and Taiwan, have also demonstrated a phenomenal capacity for industrial growth, which may initially have been stimulated by their agrarian reforms but acquired their own momentum through their aggressive penetration of world markets with labour-intensive manufactures. This has contributed to a high rate of labour absorption outside agriculture which has contained demographic pressures on the land and sustained a growth in agricultural real wages.

Few other countries with a substantial agricultural sector have been able to match the performance of the Chinese, the two Koreas and Taiwan. This has partly been due to the use of more capital-intensive technologies in their industrialization than was warranted by the factor endowments in such countries as Brazil, Mexico, India, Indonesia and Kenya. The corresponding poverty of the rural and even urban population of these countries has become a market constraint on the acceleration of the industrialization process.

In some of these newly industrializing countries, escape from the limits of the domestic market was sought in the rapid expansion of manufacturing exports. Whilst this trend has characterized the success of the East Asian newly industrializing countries, it also stimulated industrial growth in Brazil and Mexico and a number of other developing countries manufacturing exports.

The export boom of the 1960s and 1970s which sustained this pattern of export-led industrialization has run up against a slowing down in the growth of the industrialized countries. As a result the annual growth of industrial output in Brazil fell from a high of 10% between 1965 and 1980 to 0.3% in the period 1980 to 1985 (World Bank, 1987, Table 2). In Mexico industrial growth rates fell from 7.6% to 0.3% in the same period, while in Kenya they fell from 9.8% to 2%, and in Indonesia from 11.9% to 1%. Again it was only in China, the two Koreas, Taiwan and, to a lesser extent, in the more autarchic economies of

India, Pakistan and Egypt, which traditionally rely more on their large domestic markets than on the export market, that industrial growth has sustained itself despite the global recession.

It follows from the above that both market forces and technological choice have, except for the radical reform countries, put limits to the labour-absorption capacity of the industrial sector. Thus urban poverty and under-employment, along with stagnation in real wages in the urban sector, particularly in the 1980s, have become the other side of the coin to rural poverty and under-employment (ILO, 1987, Table 5.1 for trends in urban wages). The urban refuge for the rural poor has begun to reverse itself, at least in Latin America, as may be seen from the tendency of town-dwellers to seek work in neighbouring rural areas (ILO, 1987, Table 4.19). In most other regions, however, the landless and surplus labour from the agricultural sectors now congregate in fast-growing urban slums. Here agrarian reform has potential for not only improving access to rural land but also mitigating urban poverty by arresting the flight to the towns and cities of the Third World.

Target group programmes for eradicating poverty

The limited impact made in the eradication of rural poverty through the diffusion of new technology and the inadequate labour-absorption capacity of the non-agricultural sector has created a climate of mind amongst policy-makers that poverty and landlessness are likely to remain permanent features of developing countries. This has led to a number of policy palliatives and resource commitments targeted at delivering resources to the poor. These programmes range from Food for Work Programmes to various nutritional improvement, skill-enhancing and service-delivery programmes targeted at the poorest sections of the rural population. Such programmes may be incorporated into a wider Integrated Rural Development Programme (IRDP) or be specially packaged for the poorer groups. Such programmes usually tend to be underwritten by aid donors who often oscillate between their faith in the target group strategy of poverty eradication and the belief that an integrated programme of development will have both spread and trickle-down effects for the poor. Such a mix of programmes are part of the aid portfolios of donors operating in Latin America, Africa and Asia. Both the target group programmes or the IRDP model have been in use for over three decades of aid-sponsored development. In recent years, however, the imperviousness of rural poverty to the IRDP model has directed more attention to the target group approach.

The service co-operative designed to deliver credit and inputs has become the handmaiden of the IRDP. Again, special interest co-operatives for the resourceless or women have became integral to the institutional apparatus of rural development.

Historical experience, however, suggests that such targeted interventions have made no significant impact on arresting the growth of poverty and landlessness. The programmes have not been able to disturb the dynamics of immiseration discussed in this study and indeed in a massive literature on rural development. Inequitable access to power, land and other factor markets ensures that the dominant classes in the rural society will benefit from all yield-enhancing investments in the rural economy, will claim the intermediaries' share and indeed a direct share of all target groups' resources and will be best equipped to benefit from the spin-offs from all development expenditure in the rural economy. Most institutions designed to serve the rural poor, such as the service co-operatives, have been infiltrated and eventually captured by the rural elite. Very few programmes exist in the portfolios of rural developers around the world which have kept their benefits exclusively for the poor.

It is obviously not our intention to dismiss in a few paragraphs an entire range of rural development programmes targeted at the poor and the literature of evaluation these have sponsored. There are some success stories and there has been some alleviation of poverty in certain developing countries (Cassen, 1986). The inability of these programmes, however, to make an impact on the overall dynamics of rural poverty, as opposed to the circumstances of particular individuals among the rural poor obviously merits independent analysis. For our purposes it is sufficient to note that development planners, practitioners, private voluntary agencies and an army of aid bureaucrats across the world have for three decades been addressing the problem of poverty, with varying degrees of innovation and impact. But the poor are still with us, and the structural basis of poverty which has been at the core of the debate on agrarian reform remains as intractable today as it was before either reformers or planners felt they could do something to arrest its spread.

The case for agrarian reform

It is evident from our discussion earlier of the persistence of poverty and its resistance to both private and public interventions that in most developing countries the same pressures which earlier led to agrarian reforms have again surfaced as a source of concern and social tension. Under-employment of rural labour and landlessness afflict even countries which once distributed a large proportion of the agricultural land. Declining rural real wages and the persistence of rural poverty have come to characterize the lot of the minifundist farmers and landless labourers who survive as the living legacies of the inadequacy of these reforms.

Alternative areas of employment in the rural economy have failed to develop fast enough due to an inability to mobilize sufficient resources and to fashion institutions effectively to utilize those resources within the rural community. Market forces have worked to drain resources from rural areas and pre-empted the development of rural industry. Modern industry, despite its dynamic effect in promoting growth and structural change, has remained an inadequate vehicle for absorbing the landless and surplus agricultural labour to the point at which rural wages can increase and poverty be reduced.

The only countries where the rural economies have diffused technology, maximized use of the rural labour force, provided virtually universal access to the usufruct of the land, achieved sustained and equitable growth and provided an expanding market for rural and modern industry are those which have effected radical agrarian reforms. In Chapters 2, 3 and 4 we have attempted to conceptualize the link between such reforms and development and to review this relationship in its specific historical context.

There would thus appear to be overwhelming evidence to suggest that radical agrarian reforms, whether within a socialist framework, or even through a strongly supported peasant agriculture within a capitalist system, are more likely to realize equitable growth in the agricultural sector whilst arresting the growth of rural poverty. It has been argued that only by using the instrument of radical agrarian reform can differentiation within rural society be substantially eliminated. It is the persistence of differentiation which contributes to inequitable access in either linked or functionally distinct factor markets, thereby accentuating the original disparities based on land. It is argued that the minimization of this differentiation through radical agrarian reform provides for equitable access to factor markets, and indeed to the benefits from a variety of development- and aid-based programmes which contribute to the erosion of rural poverty.

In making the case for agrarian reform, we would need to discuss a number of traditional concerns about the economic difficulties which have to be faced in the post-reform phase. These concerns involve the capacity of the post-reform economy to achieve the economies of scale associated with capitalist agriculture, to sustain the diffusion of technology and to generate a marketable surplus to contribute to the growth and diversification of the economy. For the rest of this chapter we will address these arguments which have been discussed in passing in other sections of this study.

Relative productivity and the structure of production in relation to size of holdings
The case for land reform does not rest solely on considerations of social justice. A growing literature most effectively marshalled together in Berry and Cline's work 1979 has made the case for agrarian reform on grounds of efficiency. The gist of this argument is that land is more intensively utilized on smaller plots where land/labour ratios are matched more closely to ensure fuller utilization of both factors of production. Cropping patterns on smaller plots of land are such as to ensure intensive investment of labour. This has in recent years been stimulated by the green revolution, which has encouraged more use of labour as well as a capital-intensive technology. This has stimulated its adoption, particularly in Monsoon Asia, by small peasants who have managed to make their lands more productive than those of bigger landowners.

The modification of cropping patterns in smaller holdings, created by land reform, as has happened in Mexico, Bolivia and Kenya, is likely to favour food production rather than cash crops. Agrarian reforms, certainly in Latin America, have thus been associated with such a restructuring of cropping patterns, at least in the short run. There is no technical reason why this restructuring should take place on small farms; smallholder production of cash crops such as cocoa in Ghana, tea in Kenya, coffee in Costa Rica, sugar-cane in India, cotton in Pakistan, jute in Bangladesh, rubber in Malaysia, even contract growers of bananas in the Philippines, provide evidence of the efficiency of smallholdings when compared with large tea, coffee, rubber, sugar-cane or banana plantations. In these countries, cropping patterns for big as much as for smaller farmers will be dictated by a combination of market forces and policy interventions influencing relative prices of competing crops as well as factor prices and public investment decisions affecting the relative production costs of different crops. There is a considerable literature on the market responsiveness of small peasants in the Third World and evidence that failure to respond to market signals may be due to supply-side constraints such as lack of access to capital and technology.

Even if small farmers were to prefer to grow food on land hitherto reserved for highly land-intensive cattle farming, policy-makers would have to evaluate this in terms of social as much as economic priorities. It is improbable that any developing country with high levels of landlessness and under-employed agricultural labour can claim a comparative advantage for the ranch latifundias prevalent in Latin America, particularly where these countries also happen to be major food importers. Brazil, for instance, has nearly doubled its food imports from 2.5 million tons in 1974 to 4.9 million in 1985, accounting for 9% of its merchandise imports (World Bank, 1987). Despite its comparative advantage in the export of cash crops, Brazil could well afford to use idle land and labour to grow an additional five million tons of food to the benefit of both the poor and the national economy.

Within a given cropping pattern, there is considerable evidence supporting the relative efficiency of small over large holdings, and part of this efficiency points to more extensive and intensive use of land by smaller farms (World Bank, 1978; Berry and Cline, 1979, Appendix D). Berry and Cline report that in holdings of over 1,000 hectares in Brazil, only 2% of the land is under arable crops. This is not surprising if we note that properties in Brazil run to 700,000 hectares in newly developing areas such as Amazonia (Bakx, 1987). Cattle ranching and logging tend to provide cover for such extravagant uses of land.

Where land is used for arable farming, however, it is more intensively used on smallholdings where the record of multiple cropping is much better than that for larger units also engaged in arable farming. More relevant is the fact that factor productivity on small farms also tends to be more efficient (World Bank, 1978; Berry and Cline, 1979). In cases where large farms appear to have higher land yields this is because of heavy capital investment in mechanized agriculture, and usually happens because capital is priced below its market value, whether in Pakistan, Brazil or the Philippines (Berry and Cline, 1979; Khan, 1981). This encourages inappropriate and less efficient use of capital, when the use of abundant labour and much less capital and land would have achieved the same results at a significantly lower cost.

Berry and Cline's conclusion that a redistribution of land from large to smaller holdings will be conducive to the expansion of productive forces thus deserves our attention. They estimate gains in national agricultural output from land redistribution to smallholdings to be in the region of 25% in Brazil (as much as 79.5% in North-East Brazil), 28% in Colombia, 19% in India, 10% in Pakistan, 23% in the Philippines and 28% in Malaysia. However academic such an exercise may be, it is a measure of the potential productivity gains from agrarian reform. Agrarian reform is thus one policy intervention where equity and growth would appear to be reconcilable.

Capturing economies of scale following land reform

Where significant economies of scale exist for particular crops, it does not follow that in the wake of an agrarian reform such economies cannot be realized through institutional measures. Economies of scale associated with access to capital, procurement of inputs, marketing of the crop and development of the infrastructure can and have been achieved within the collectivist format in the socialist countries and within co-operatives for different factor markets as in East Asia, and indeed even in a number of non-egalitarian reform countries.

Where the old estates are kept intact, as in Cuba, the nationalized plantations in coastal Peru, *haciendas* in Chile or the *autogestion* estates taken over from the *colons* in Algeria, agrarian reforms have not modified the original technology. Berry and Cline would indeed argue that even such state farms should be reduced in scale, as is happening today in Algeria, or should be redistributed to individual households. In countries such as Angola and Mozambique, the retention of the large settler holdings in large state farms, in a changed managerial situation, was counter-productive, and a distribution of land to smallholders might have been more sensible. Similarly, in Peru the attempt to combine collective cultivation with smallholdings in the *haciendas* taken over in the highlands was an unviable arrangement and the redistribution of the entire estate into smallholdings would have been more efficient. The economies of scale could have been achieved in co-operative support and marketing services to the post-reform holdings, as in South Korea, Taiwan and Japan.

The added hazard of converting large *haciendas* into state enterprises which usually employ the original workers on the farms is that these same workers become an obstacle to giving land rights to other landless households in adjacent areas. It is those workers who thus preserve the inefficient and inappropriate land/labour ratios of the former *hacendados* and acquire the privileges of a new exploiting class employing labour from adjacent lands. This happened in Peru when the coastal sugar *haciendas* were nationalized and again in Chile when large estates were kept intact after the reform.

The question of the marketable surplus

In Chapter 3 we reviewed the Soviet debate on the marketable surplus. That original debate still continues to tantalize policy-makers reviewing the case for agrarian reform. The argument still holds that an agrarian reform which restructures the cropping pattern away from production for the market to production for domestic consumption will prejudice the rate of growth and the diversification of the economy. This will condemn the economy to stagnation at low levels of consumption and technology. This argument is, however, predicated on the assumption that cropping patterns as opposed to land-use patterns will be restructured in the wake of reform and that land productivity can most effectively be improved by extracting a surplus from the producers and converting it into capital for re-investment.

Our discussion in Chapters 3 to 6 of the nature and impact of agrarian reforms does not lend support to the stagnation thesis. As we have observed, cropping patterns have been kept intact where the original estates have been preserved. In Algeria, however, changes in cropping patterns on *colon* land did take place. This was dictated less by the direction of the reform than the erosion of protected markets for *colon* agriculture provided by metropolitan France when Algeria was deemed to be an integrated part of France (King, 1977). The loss of the French market and consequential restructuring of cropping patterns thus helped reduce (in addition to the impact of rising oil and gas exports) primary products from 39% of the share of Algeria's merchandise exports in 1965 to a negligible figure in 1985 (World Bank, 1987, Table 2). In Mozambique, Angola, even Nicaragua and, to an extent, Sri Lanka, primary exports were also reduced in the post-reform phase. In these cases the problem was less due to restructuring of production than an inability to sustain production, which inevitably caused a fall in exports and an erosion of the marketable surplus from agriculture.

In most other cases, as in Bolivia, Mexico and Kenya, agrarian reforms redistributing lands to smallholders did not, except temporarily, interfere with crop production, and once the new relations of production had stabilized, agricultural production improved in the 1960s. In other cases, however, such as Zimbabwe, while the overall production trends prior to the 1992 drought remained indeterminate, the marketable surplus has contracted.

In countries outside Latin America and Africa, relations of production were not disturbed because the agrarian reforms in effect left production in the hands of the tillers. Cotton in Egypt or Pakistan, sugar-cane in India, jute in Bangladesh, rice in Thailand, rubber in Malaysia or coconuts in the Philippines continued to be cultivated by the same farmers who tilled the land as share-croppers. This same class, not deemed to be owners or possessing security of tenure, tended to leave their cropping patterns undisturbed and continued to be no less responsive to the relative prices of different crops in the market than commercial farmers. Indeed, they were probably much more responsive since a small-scale sugar-cane grower or cotton planter could switch to food or cash crops much more smoothly than a sugar-cane planter with all his investments tied up in the growing of cane for his sugar mill. It would thus appear that the marketable surplus for cash crops remained more sensitive to market forces than it did to agrarian reforms, and that if anything a reform which vested land in smallholders made commercial agriculture more, rather than less, sensitive to market forces.

The tendency for exports of the marketable surplus to remain relatively undisturbed after a reform is less valid for food crops than it is for cash crops. Whilst some Third World countries, such as Pakistan and Thailand for rice and Argentina for wheat, remain significant exporters of food crops, the bulk of Third World countries only generate a marketable surplus of food directed at the home market essentially to meet the need for wage goods in their urban sector. This, indeed, was at the heart of the debate in the USSR between Preobrazhensky and Bukharin (Mitra, 1977), and the issue continues to arouse concern over the negative impact of agrarian reforms. It is argued that a reform which eliminates or reduces the need to generate a surplus in order to meet the crop share of the landlord will reduce the aggregate marketable surplus. It is unusual for government land taxes to make up for the landlord's share, so that after a reform a much larger proportion of the crop stays with the former tenant, who may consume most of it if he and his family have been running at below subsistence levels previously. Similarly where land is redistributed from a *hacendado*/capitalist farmer, who used to extract a surplus from his *colonatos* for sale in the market, and handed over to a peasant, the marketable surplus may well contract to vanishing point since the peasant only wants primarily to meet his basic needs for food. In such a situation the needs of the urban market, and indeed of a growing class of agricultural workers who include many food-deficit households, will have to be met from food imports.

This restructuring of food production from the market to the household needs to be more fully examined in the specific historic context of particular countries, but a short-cut to assessing this tendency would be to see whether food imports have been rising in relation to total food availability. This tendency reflects the inability of the marketable surplus to keep pace with the demand for food. In practice, however, the food gap, as measured by imports, may be wider since imports may be less than the actual food gap due to a country's inability to import food. The actual food gap based on a normal level of access to foreign exchange would need to be computed from 'normal-year' levels. We would, however, need to differentiate between the contribution made by an absolute decline in per capita production of food and a decline in the marketable surplus in determining the size of the food gap. It is, however, quite plausible that the decline in food production per capita may have to be compensated for by a rise in imports. This would simply indicate the failure of food production to keep pace with the rise in population. However a food gap which opens up, even when food production per capita is increasing, is more likely to be reflected by the failure of the marketable surplus to keep pace with food production. This may, of course, again reflect an overall increase in per capita food consumption and/or an increased retention of food within the producing household or unit.

For the purposes of the study we may make a rather crude assumption that where a rise in food production per capita coincides with a significant rise in imports there must have been a decline in the marketable surplus for that country. Using this measure, with all its identifiable conceptual inadequacies, we may look at the groups of countries who have reduced/increased their food imports between 1974–84 in a contrary direction to the per capita food production trend. The review is presented in Table 4.

Table 4
Structure of the Economy, Growth in Production and Cereal Imports, in Agrarian Reform Countries

	(1) % of Rural Population/Total Population		(2) % Agricultural Labour Force/Total Labour Force		(3) % Agricultural GDP/Total GDP		(4) Index of Food Production Per Capita (1974=100)	(5) Cereal Imports (in million metric tons)		(6) Average Agricultural Growth Rate per annum %	
	1965	1985	1965	1980	1965	1985	1982-84	1974	1984	1965-73	1973-84
A. Radical Agrarian Reforms											
1. China	82	78	81	74	39	33	128	9.8	15.2	2.8	4.9
2. Vietnam	84	80	79	68	N.A.	N.A.	123	1.9	0.4	N.A.	N.A.
3. North Korea	55	37	57	43	64* (1946)	18 (1965)	113	1.1	0.2	N.A.	N.A.
4. Cuba	42	29	33	24	18*	13	129	1.6	2.1	N.A.	N.A.
5. South Korea	68	36	55	36	38	14	—	2.7	6.3	2.9	1.7
6. Taiwan	—	—	—	—	—	—	—	—	—	—	—
7. Ethiopia	92	85	66	80	58	54	100	9.1	0.5	2.1	1.2
B. Inegalitarian Reforms With Social Transition											
8. Mexico	45	31	50	37	14	11	104	2.9	8.5	5.4	3.4
9. Bolivia	60	56	54	46	23	27	84	0.2	0.3	3.5	1.1
10. Chile	28	17	27	17	9	N.A.	84	1.7	1.0	-1.1	3.4
11. Peru	48	32	50	40	18	11	102	0.6	1.2	2.0	1.2
12. Nicaragua	57	44	57	47	25	23	78	0.04	0.1	2.8	1.4
13. Egypt	58	54	55	46	29	20	91	3.9	8.6	2.6	2.5
14. Iraq	49	30	50	30	18	N.A.	85	0.9	4.5	1.7	N.A.

15.	Algeria	62	57	57	31	15	8	79	1.8	4.2	2.4	4.2
16.	Syria	60	51	52	32	29	22	123	0.3	1.9	-0.7	6.8
17.	Mozambique	95	81	87	85	N.A.	35	73	0.06	0.4	N.A.	N.A.
C.	**Inegalitarian Reforms Without Social Transition**											
18.	Tunisia	60	44	49	35	22	17	84	0.3	1.1	6.6	1.9
19.	Kenya	91	80	86	81	35	31	82	0.015	0.6	6.2	3.5
20.	Zimbabwe	86	73	79	73	18	13	69	0.056	0.3	N.A.	1.1
21.	Bangladesh	94	82	84	75	53	50	99	1.9	2.1	0.4	3.1
22.	India	81	75	73	70	47	31	110	5.3	2.2	3.7	2.3
23.	Pakistan	76	71	60	55	40	25	104	1.3	0.3	4.7	3.0
24.	Sri Lanka	80	79	56	53	28	27	125	0.95	0.7	2.7	4.1
25.	Indonesia	84	75	71	57	56	24	120	1.9	1.9	4.8	3.7
26.	Thailand	87	62	62	71	35	17	115	0.1	0.15	5.2	3.7
27.	Philippines	68	61	58	52	26	27	107	0.8	0.96	4.1	4.0
28.	Costa Rica	62	56	47	31	24	20	87	0.1	0.14	7.0	1.9
29.	El Salvador	61	57	59	43	N.A.	19	88	0.075	0.2	3.6	0.4
30.	Guatemala	66	58	64	57	40	N.A.	101	0.14	0.14	5.8	1.9
31.	Honduras	74	61	68	61	18	27	99	0.05	0.13	2.2	3.6
32.	Panama	56	50	46	32	27	9	99	0.063	0.185	3.4	2.1
33.	Ecuador	63	48	55	39	30	14	89	0.15	0.37	3.9	1.6
34.	Colombia	46	33	45	34	7	20	104	0.5	0.8	4.0	3.5
35.	Venezuela	28	15	30	16		8	88	1.3	2.7	4.5	2.4

Sources:
1. All Countries: World Bank, 1986.
2. North Korea: McCormack & Gittings, 1977.
3. Cuba: Brundenius (1984).

Looking at Table 4, we observe that 10 out of 36 countries which enacted agrarian reforms of varying sorts increased food imports whilst food production per capita increased. This includes four out of eight countries which enacted radical reforms. China increased its food production per capita to 128 in 1984 (1974–76 = 100) but its imports increased from 9.8 million tons in 1974 to 15.2 million in 1984, though imports fell to 10.4 million in 1985. Cuba, which increased production to an index of 129, increased food imports from 1.6 to 2.1 million tons. South Korea increased food production to 169 but increased imports from 2.7 million tons in 1974 to 6.35 million tons in 1984. It is only in Vietnam and North Korea that increases in production were matched by quite sizeable cuts in imports. This suggests that the marketable surplus must have increased to compensate for the fall in imports. In the case of North Korea this cut in imports still left calorie intake in 1983 at 127% of requirements, but in Vietnam calorie intake was only 93% of requirements, so that the cut in imports was not fully compensated by an increase in the marketable surplus.

Other countries where cuts in imports coincided with a fall in food production per capita include Tanzania and Chile, where import cuts would appear to have derived from balance of payments constraints. For most other countries, improved or declining food production appeared consistent with a fall or a rise in imports. There are, however, variations in the consistency of the match. India, for example, increased its per capita output to only 110 in 1984, but reduced its imports from 5.3 to 1.6 million tons between 1974 and 1984. A quantitative analysis of the relationship between the surplus, food production and imports would make such conclusions rather more rigorous.

It is noticeable that countries with radical reforms such as China, Cuba and South Korea, would appear in recent years to have experienced a contraction in their marketable surplus. This indicates that higher consumption was in part absorbed on the farm, leaving imports to meet the needs of the urban sector. The Soviet model of a post-reform collectivized agriculture being forced to meet the food demands of the industrial sector, notwithstanding its own lacklustre production performance and rural consumption needs, thus would not appear to apply to the radical reformers. This tendency to let the surplus of the land reform beneficiaries in these countries be retained within the farm is consistent with the favourable policy bias towards the farmer in these countries.

One may conclude that whilst in countries which have experienced agrarian reform the verdict on their capacity to sustain food production per capita is mixed, there is a discernible tendency for the marketable surplus to contract as measured by the increase in food imports. Newly benefited owners of small farm holdings thus prefer to eat more and, even when collectivized, may continue to do so, notwithstanding any broader national claim on them to make additional food available to the rest of the population. This hypothesis may indeed be borne out in the case of Ethiopia where recent famines appear to be localized phenomena aggravated by an inability to extract a marketable surplus of food from less affected areas populated by minifundist land reform beneficiaries.

Diffusing improved technology
We have already observed that, at least in Monsoon Asia, there is ample evidence to establish the relative efficiency of small farmers' use of the new technologies compared to large farmers. Fragmentary evidence for Latin America suggests that smallholders are not noticeably less efficient than rich farmers in using new technologies. Where the technology is divisible and/or supported by institutional intervention in both technology diffusion and manipulation of the market regime in favour of small farmers, there is nothing to suggest that large farmers are inherently more efficient adapters than small farmers. In the case of most crops, appropriate technology is not particularly associated with large farms. In cases where there is an association, as for instance in livestock farming, collective institutions or even service co-operatives could compensate for smallholders' lack of access to economies of scale. The collective could provide investments for improving livestock yield and processing its output, as is evident from the experience of Cuba and China. The experience of the famous Anand Dairy Co-operatives in India shows that small-scale livestock ownership can be matched by co-operative investment to service the farmers and process and market their output. The notion that large livestock latifundias are the only way to rear cattle is more a reflection of how particular power configurations limit technology choice than a measure of appropriate technology.

Agrarian reforms which go beyond the mere redistribution of land to bring about in addition a transformation in the social and economic circumstances of the small farmer or landless households have at their disposal appropriate institutional and policy interventions which can effectively compensate the technology-induced economies of scale associated with large holdings. Since these large holdings traditionally tend to use land and capital inefficiently – largely because of their cheap cost, that is itself often artificially induced and land and capital occasionally illegally appropriated – access to these factors of production and interventions to maintain technology diffusion should not unduly tax the imagination of policy-makers. It is, however, inexcusable to create a class of smallholders, leave them to fend for themselves in the imperfect factor markets for capital and commodities, and then attribute their failure to do so to the diseconomies of minifundism.

Institutions and policies to enhance the efficiency of agrarian reforms

Agrarian reforms on their own create the basis for a more equitable access to land, and through this access to land to related factor markets and public resources. Thus a measure of the success of a reform lies in the degree of equity in access to land realized by the particular reform and its success in eliminating socio-political differentiation within the peasantry. This category of poor or small peasants cannot be left to stagnate in a state of technological stasis, low investment and productivity. The principal tasks of the post-reform phase must therefore be to create a collective consciousness amongst the land reform beneficiaries, which is not the same as putting them in collective farms. This newly enfranchized class of producers, unless they are to devour each other in the market place, will have to co-operate to create and diffuse technology, have equitable access to capital and build up their bargaining power in the market for their products. This collectivist vision may be realized in a system of small-holder agriculture or through collective planning of production and labour use. Whilst the move towards collectivism may in part be due to levels of political consciousness which determine how far different communities will be motivated by personal, in place of collective, goals, our review of historical experience suggests that the choice may be dictated as much by demography and geography. In societies with adverse land–labour ratios, the collective appears to be a more efficient mechanism for fuller utilization of labour and in using the socially appropriated surplus to ensure full employment of labour and resources within the community. This may or may not lead to less efficient use of capital, depending on the appropriate market signals and/or managerial efficiency of the collective.

In societies where land resources are sufficient to ensure reasonably full utilization of household labour on small family-sized holdings, there would appear to be less need to collectivize production and labour use. The ideal mix would appear to be to let households retain direct attachment with the land they cultivate but to socialize their surplus labour in relation to land size for building up social investment to promote improvements in both household productivity and consumption of collective goods. The new model of Household Responsibility in China may seek to reconcile the need for individual incentive with collective responsibility, but may be going too far in the direction of the individual with unforeseen consequences for the preservation of collective wealth and indeed for the return of differentiation within the peasantry.

The creation of appropriate institutions to compensate for economies of scale of large farms needs to be backed up by policy interventions in the realm of pricing and resource allocation supportive of the land reform beneficiary. We have observed in Chapters 3 and 4 how such positive interventions characterized the treatment of the farm sector in the radical reform countries. The land reform beneficiaries will need to be given incentive prices to sustain production rather than be forced to surrender more of their surplus, whether through taxation or the manipulation of the terms of trade. They will need an allocative regime which uses public resources to build up the rural infrastructure, provides credit and supplies critical inputs. These are, above all, allocative decisions where the state rather than the market will have to take political decisions sensitive to the needs of farmers. This is a situation more likely to exist where the power of the state has been underwritten by the support of poor peasants.

The market regime within which the land reform beneficiaries thrive will itself be sensitive to the policies of the state outside agriculture. An economically enfranchized peasantry retaining the benefits of its own productivity and collective investments provides a dynamic market for the non-agricultural sector. To the extent that agrarian reform creates a class of small farmers it creates a demand for the produce of rural and local industry. Peasants wear and use hand-woven products, use equipment, intermediate inputs and finished products which can be made in rural workshops or local industry. It is the *hacendado* who wears imported Gucci shoes, drives a Mercedes, air-conditions his home, uses large General Motors tractors and visits New York or Paris several times a year. Agrarian reform has the potential for changing the nature of consumption and hence the structure of demand for non-agricultural goods and services. The changed structure of demand will be more indigenous in its use of resources and production and potentially less capital-intensive in its use and choice of technology.

Obviously the scope for realizing the benefits of an involuted development strategy will vary from country to country. What is feasible for countries with large domestic markets, such as the countries of South Asia, Indonesia, Egypt, Nigeria, Brazil or Mexico, whose potential may be more fully tapped by an egalitarian agrarian reform, will not be the same for Nicaragua, Zimbabwe or Sri Lanka. A development strategy designed to serve the needs of a more egalitarian social order created by agrarian reform is likely to be more conducive to utilizing indigenous resources and skills developed in an economic culture derived from the available resource base of a country. This applies to Benin as much as to Bangladesh (Sobhan and Islam, 1987). This argument can be made without prejudice to a strategy which promotes exports to generate the foreign exchange needed to underwrite a more self-reliant development strategy.

8. Conclusion: The Political Economy of Agrarian Reform

The scope for reform

The compelling logic which underlies the need for radical agrarian reform is, unfortunately, hardly likely to promote such reforms. The central argument of this study has been that the nature and impact of agrarian reform originate in the evolving balance of power within rural society and beyond it in the state. We therefore need to make a realistic appraisal of the prevailing balance of power in contemporary Third World countries and to relate this to the available land resources which may be incorporated in an agrarian reform. In this chapter we will look briefly at the varying circumstances of countries in relation to land available for distribution and then assess the nature and scope for the mobilization necessary to realize a shift in the balance of power sufficient to effect a radical agrarian reform. We will in conclusion review the possible implications of a failure to effect such reforms.

The availability of land for distribution

Within our framework of analysis we have emphasized the importance of egalitarian reforms in ensuring not just more equitable access to land but also to other factor markets. The elimination of an intermediate dominant class thus becomes an end in itself for a reform and can be carried through irrespective of the land to labour ratio in a particular country.

Highly inequitable access to land and the persistence of large tracts of land concentrated in the hands of a small number of owners lends itself more readily to redistributive reforms than would a reform programme to reduce a 10-hectare ceiling to three hectares. This is obviously a political rather than an economic issue. The more people are affected by a reform, the more difficult it becomes to carry through a reform except as part of a more general upheaval of the social order as occurred in China, Vietnam, North Korea and Ethiopia. Targeting a small number of large landholders sitting on latifundias is more feasible but by no means easy, as is evident in the case of Brazil. Where this class is made up of generals, senior civil servants and the urban rich who monopolize state power, its capacity to frustrate land reform, acting both within the law and outside it, is formidable. Making allowances for inter-state variations in the distribution of power, it remains valid that agrarian reforms, in countries which still have large tracts of land within a small number of holdings, is more feasible than where land is held in relatively smaller holdings, even by the upper echelons of landowners.

Latin America

Within this perspective further agrarian reforms are obviously more plausible in Latin America than in most other parts of the Third World. Looking at Table 1 we can match measures of land concentration with degrees of landlessness and this suggests a discernible coincidence between land concentration and landlessness. In Latin America agrarian reforms in Brazil would appear to be at the top of anyone's agenda because it is here that high levels of land-poverty, urban congestion and vast latifundias co-exist. If all estates in Brazil above 500 hectares were expropriated, some 55.5% of the nation's farm land would be available for redistribution. This would be more than adequate for giving viable plots of land to all landless households as well as those with holdings of less than two hectares. However much of this land would be uncultivated pasture or forest land which would have some effect on Brazil's commitment to large-scale livestock operations. The conversion of this land to arable farming and to smaller size livestock units could potentially transform the social and economic landscape in Brazil, perhaps with positive benefits for agricultural production.

If Bolivia, in the post-reform period in 1970, expropriated all holdings above 1,000 hectares this would have affected only 3,000 owners; if they were permitted to retain 1,000 hectares per household this would still leave 18 million hectares for distribution. If we applied a ceiling of 30 hectares for redistribution, this would enable 600,000 households to have access to farm land, compared to the 289,000 which benefited from the 1954 reforms. This numbers game, however, conceals the fact that much of this surplus land in Bolivia is located in mountainous areas and is suitable only for raising livestock. Thus some assessment of the capacity of potential land reform beneficiaries either to crop this land or use it for pasture would have to be attempted.

Such large tracts of land, held in a few holdings, remain a common feature in other Latin American countries. Thus in Mexico, if a ceiling of 1,000 hectares was put on post-reform holdings, some 42 million hectares could be expropriated from 10,000 holdings (on 1970 figures). If these were left with 1,000 hectares each, 32 million hectares would still be available for redistribution. In Peru a new land ceiling of 1,000 hectares would leave six million hectares for appropriation from 1,500 holdings. Allowing for a 1,000 hectare retention limit this would still leave 4.5 million hectares or 25% of all land for redistribution. In Chile, however, new land reform would need to go down to a family farm size of 20 hectares if any land is to be netted for redistribution. A 20-hectare ceiling would net around 8.6 million hectares from 18,200 holdings. A move from what are essentially capitalist holdings of around 80 hectares to a household-based holding would imply a change in relations of production.

This exercise could be carried out on paper for the rest of Latin America, where in virtually every country large tracts of land, held in holdings of 1,000 hectares and above, or in rare cases 100 hectares and above, are tempting targets for agrarian reformers. In all such cases, however, the reforms would usually strike at large corporate holdings or *haciendas* engaged in growing export crops or in ranching operations, using the most capital- and land-intensive technologies available. In most cases this class of *hacendados* have diversified their investments into industry, finance and banking and are an integral part of the ruling oligarchies of these countries. Agrarian reform would thus demand a social revolution hitting not just at the balance of power in the countryside but also at the prevailing configurations of state power.

Furthermore, an assault on large capitalist agricultural holdings would have implications for the efficiency of the farm sector and the size of the marketable surplus. It would, however, require a more careful country-by-country analysis of land-use by size of land holding to ascertain what proportion of these holdings were uncultivated and/or uncultivable without sizeable investment in land development. Where land in use is to be appropriated then the impact of a reform on cropping patterns would merit review as to its production, export and savings effect. If a large soya-bean plantation is taken over and used to grow millet in smallholdings, the socio-economics of such a trade-off will merit examination. However where a 1,000-hectare coffee, banana, or sugar *hacienda* is broken up into 200 family holdings of five hectares, the relative economics of smallholder cultivation may well be more productive for the economy and without prejudice to export or savings (Berry and Cline, 1979).

Latin America, with some exceptions such as Chile, thus emerges as perhaps the only region where agrarian reform is still feasible within the prevailing relations of production. Capitalist farms can still be operated, and probably more efficiently, on holdings of 500 hectares as much as on units of 5,000 hectares. To let a corporate entity own half a million hectares of Amazonia or 100,000 hectares of Bolivian farm land is not the touchstone of capitalist agriculture. Thus the scope for creating a class of medium-sized farmers owning 100–500 hectares could net sizeable acreage for redistribution as we have indicated.

Africa

Outside Latin America there are few countries with large estates presenting inviting targets to be carved up. The few remaining white settler estates in Kenya, the still considerable tracts of land held by white settlers in Zimbabwe and, of course, the large estates of South Africa's white population remain the last of Africa's open land frontiers. At least in Kenya and Zimbabwe such lands are already in the process of being transferred. As we observed for Zimbabwe, the recent political reconfiguration of the regime into a de facto one-party state guided by a populist ideology is hardly compatible with large, white settler capitalist farms. This became clear in 1992 with the Zimbabwean government accelerating plans to expropriate a large proportion of remaining white-owned agricultural estates. This could leave the state with large tracts of fertile farm land for distribution. The key question will be whether to distribute these as individual peasant holdings or to farm them in various commercial/collectivist tenures. The answer may ultimately be dictated as much by the pace of the settler withdrawal as by the ideology of the Mugabe regime. To what extent the pressure from the indigenous population for acquiring these lands is weaker in Zimbabwe than in Kenya is unclear. If so, the decision in the former may well be top-down rather than the product of peasant activism. In Kenya, certainly, the growing inequalities in access to land could carry the seeds of peasant mobilization, but more information about the tribal basis of politics and land access in Kenya is needed to make a definitive analysis of such a mobilization.

Elsewhere in Africa, such as in the francophone regions and Zaire, the corporate holdings of metropolitan capital do not monopolize land, which still remains available on a sufficient scale to cater for the land-hunger of the African peasantry.

The Middle East

In the Middle East the one country in which large holdings could be re-apportioned is Morocco; in all other countries of North Africa the transition to capitalist, statist or household tenures has been largely realized.

Even in Syria and Iraq, despite the large holdings retained by capitalist farmers, there is sufficient appropriated land which is being inadequately farmed and no real pressure from an aspirant class of peasant cultivators to seek more land. The operative transition would be through a conversion into state farms of the limited number of capitalist farms in operation.

In Egypt, however, there is a sizeable constituency of the landless and land-poor and enough land held by rich peasants or capitalist farmers who hire in labour to sustain a new generation of reforms. If the objective is to recreate an agrarian system of peasants, as appeared to underlie the objectives of the Nasserite reforms, then a land ceiling of around 10 feddans (about 10 acres) would leave around 2.2 million feddans in holdings of above 10 feddans for distribution (King, 1977). Assuming that there were 100,000 such large farmers, each of whom could retain 10 feddans, then around 1.2 million feddans would be available for redistribution. If lots of five feddans were set up for redistribution, some 200,000 households would become beneficiaries of the reforms, compared to the three million households identified in 1965 as having holdings of 0.5 feddan and below and the even larger number of landless households which survived even after the reforms of the 1960s.

Since 1965 Egypt has experienced an annual rate of population growth of 2.2% between 1965 and 1973 and 2.6% between 1973 and 1985; between 1965 and 1984 the country's rural population increased to 26 million. Assuming an average household size of five, this gives us 5.3 million rural households compared to 3.2 million in 1965. This suggests that a 10-feddan ceiling would distribute 18.6% of the land, but to only 3.8% of rural households. These numbers unfortunately tell us nothing of the quality of the land and what part of the 1.2 million feddans declared surplus would be potentially cultivable. Even if we make the extravagant assumption that all of it is potentially cultivable, a new reform would still have only a marginal impact on the landless and land-poor. This suggests that in Egypt a radical reform would be needed to effect a change in relations of production of the Chinese variety, with collective use of land and more important, of labour, if access to land is to be made significantly more widespread than it is today.

Asia

A meaningful radical reform in South Asia, in Bangladesh, Sri Lanka and India would need to move along the Chinese path if sufficiently large proportions of the rural population would hope to be affected by such a reform. Possibly in Pakistan the basis of a peasant agriculture may appear feasible. If we set a ceiling for Pakistan of 10 hectares, then some 8.36 million hectares (as of 1980) would fall above this ceiling and be eligible for distribution. Assuming an agricultural population of 40.38 million and five members to a household, this would mean some 8.1 million agricultural households. Of these some 9.2%, or 745,000 households, already have holdings of more than 10 hectares. If each of these retained 10 hectares, only 0.91 million hectares would be available for redistribution to the rest. If a conservative ceiling of two hectares was set as the unit of distribution, this would still benefit only 5.6% of the households and only distribute less than 10% of cultivable land. This illustrates the limits of land reform even in an agrarian system with substantial areas of land concentrated in large holdings.

The limits to surplus land derived from even relatively low ceilings set at 7.5–10 acres for South-East Asia as well as for South Asia will in fact net little land relative to the numbers of potential claimants. In Indonesia and the Philippines the rich farmers holding paddy lands would appear as a whole to be beyond the reach of a ceiling type redistributive land reform.

As in South Asia, so in the South-East Asian countries, there are no doubt a fair number of clandestine holdings by families which retain lands under family control that are well above the permitted ceilings set by an earlier generation of land reforms. This is particularly so in India and Pakistan where ceilings were set low enough to encourage evasion by recalcitrant but powerful zamindars or aspirant capitalists. This South Asian case may be contrasted with Latin America and the Middle East where ceilings were set sufficiently high not to antagonize the entrepreneurial energies and power-hunger of the landowners.

Despite much writing and public rhetoric on the subject, very few such evasions of the land reform ceiling have in practice been detected in any Asian country. This reflects the capacity of the landowning classes to manipulate the local officials entrusted with enforcing the land reform laws, as well as to use the law courts which in these countries have traditionally been an instrument to serve the affluent classes. Under the protection of the law, landowners can re-apportion lands within their family or clients, often in breach of laws forbidding such antedated redistribution of land. Such is the inherited and undisturbed power of this class that such evasions can pass undetected or more serious, undisturbed, since every poor peasant or tenant in the area will know the reality of who controls the land. Thus, as we have observed earlier, data on landownership, as opposed to data on land holding, remains much more inaccessible and where available may conceal the full inequalities in title to land.

However, information about who owns what land, and how much, is of only academic interest given a conservative balance of power, and it can only be elicited and acted upon if a new power dispensation vests the right to unearth and re-appropriate surplus lands in the hands of potential land reform beneficiaries. We have observed that in the radical agrarian reform countries this is precisely what set their reforms apart from countries experiencing non-egalitarian reforms. Whether in China, Vietnam, North Korea, Japan or Ethiopia, the prime movers in the distributive process were poor peasants. Even in South Korea the political empowerment of the poor peasant during the brief episode of control by North Korean cadres during the Korean War created a political consciousness which ensured enforcement of what was already radical land reform legislation.

The scope for tenancy reforms

Whilst the scope for readily accessing surplus lands for further redistribution remains limited for most of Monsoon Asia, there is considerable scope for effecting reforms which convert the tiller of tenanted land into its owner. Although, relative to the need and scope for land distribution, much land was not distributed in the 1972 agrarian reforms in the Philippines, large numbers of share tenants did become owners or acquired fixed leaseholds of the land they tilled at low rentals (Sobhan, 1983). In India, the agrarian reforms effected by successive Marxist governments in the state of Kerala went a long way to making former tenants into owners (Herring, 1985), while in the state of West Bengal another Marxist government managed to secure fixed leaseholds for share-croppers, thereby significantly enhancing their security of tenure (Ghose, 1983). Less successful attempts at providing security of tenure and reducing the crop share paid by tenants in Pakistan and Bangladesh suggest that a mere belief in effecting reforms may not actually widen access to land in practice (Herring, 1985; Siddiqui, 1979).

Tenancy reforms obviously have more of a future in Asia than redistributive reforms. The Filipino, Keralan or West Bengal tenancy reforms are entirely feasible in the rest of India, Bangladesh, Pakistan, Sri Lanka, Indonesia and Thailand. Efficiency gains may be more illusory, since in Asian agriculture sufficient evidence has accumulated to indicate that share-croppers are no less efficient in their use of tenanted land than small owners, (Khan, 1981; Hossain, 1987). This is due to the fact that most tenants in Asia today are small peasants who rent in land so that there is no particular reason why they should farm tenanted land less efficiently than owned land. Since small farmers rent in land to ensure their subsistence, and they have to generate a surplus to pay for the use of the land, the need to extract the most out of the land is very strong.

The real problem in effecting tenancy reforms has always been the evasive action taken by landowners at even the whisper of such a reform and the South Asian experience is replete with experiences of anticipatory eviction of sitting tenants and the resumption of lands for self-cultivation (Khan, 1981; Herring, 1985; Siddiqui, 1979). Here again the balance of power has to tilt sufficiently within the polity to frustrate such evasions; the Filipino reform, therefore, had a better record than that in South Asia due to the Marcos regime's determination to weaken the base of the landowning politicians.

The more enduring problem for serious tenancy reform is, however, the problem of the small landowner. We have observed in the Philippines that the ubiquity of this class seriously limited the scope of land distribution. In South Asia there are many members of the urban working class and petit bourgeoisie who rent out land whilst they seek a living in the cities. Many poor peasants now rent out their land and seek more rewarding wage employment. An aggressively pursued land-to-the-tiller strategy, as was implemented in Kerala, may in fact dispossess the weak and even make new owners of the rich and the middle peasants renting in land (Herring, 1985).

Having taken note of this potential inequity in a strategy of making all share tenants into the owners of their land, such a reform would appear to be a more easily targeted reform programme, with little disruptive effect on production and cropping patterns. It would, however, not necessarily be any more politically feasible than a redistributive reform, particularly where large numbers of small landlords would be affected.

Preconditions for further land reform

The conclusions to be derived from the arguments enumerated at the outset of this study and elaborated in our review of the variety of national experiences in earlier chapters, is that any significant new land reform, whether in those countries discussed here or in those which have remained exposed only to an agrarian transition enacted through the market mechanism, as in Brazil, will remain dependent on further changes in the balance of power in the rural community. Such changes in the balance of power, we have argued, arose only in specific historical circumstances where the mobilization of the peasantry and/or exogenously induced changes in the domestic power balance created the preconditions for agrarian transformation in particular countries. The intensity of this change in the power balance dictated the nature of the reform and its outcome.

Political feasibility

Having reviewed a variety of reforms in terms of their effectiveness in reducing differentiations within the peasantry, or at least containing the accentuation of such differentiations, we have identified the need and scope for agrarian reforms in a number of developing countries, most of which have already been through a phase of agrarian reform. However it remains appropriate to analyse the political feasibility of a new generation of agrarian reforms and to identify the potential for political mobilization needed to realize such reforms.

The political mobilization needed to realize radical reforms in the contemporary developing world remains elusive. Indeed, the earlier generation of partial reforms which effected a social transition from a class of absentee landowners/traditional *hacendados* to a more numerous class of resident capitalist farmers or rich peasants has itself become the principal political barrier to further reform. This new class controls the electoral system in what remain at best highly formalistic democracies, where such exist, and monopolizes access to state and local power. The increased patronage at their disposal enables them to divide and control politically the landless and land-poor, just as their monopoly over resources other than land reinforces their economic control over the poor peasant.

The rare cases in the 1970s in which new agrarian reforms were enacted emerged out of peasant mobilizations ending in the overthrow of a long-established social order (Ethiopia) and political order (Nicaragua). Whilst the Nicaraguan agrarian reforms may have come to a standstill with the electoral defeat of the Sandinista regime, the crisis of production as well as overthrow of the Mengistu regime in Ethiopia has placed the permanence of the reforms also in that country into question.

Such rare mobilizations tend to erupt only in countries where a narrowly-based exploiting class, whose power is epitomized in a visible target such as the head of the state, dominates rural life. Haile Selassie in Ethiopia and Somoza in Nicaragua were obvious targets of such a mobilization. Such targets are, however, few and far between at the present time. In Latin America the last of this type of regime is probably in Paraguay. There the oldest *caudillo* of the area, Stroessner, presided from 1954 over a highly inegalitarian land system; in 1981 the gini-coefficient for landholdings was 0.94, the most inequitable land distribution in any country in the world for which data is available. Stroessner's relatively recent overthrow as a result of a coup from within the regime has not, however, threatened the power base of the oligarchy which dominates Paraguay, and we have no reason to expect any assault on the prevailing patterns of landownership in that country. In other parts of Latin America where landownership is still highly inequitable, as for instance in Brazil, political power has been diffused not only in rural society but also in the state. The peasantry is in fact now a minority group in Brazil; in 1985 only 27% of Brazil's population lived in rural areas and just 31% of the labour force was engaged in agriculture (World Bank, 1987). Indeed in 1980, 17.7% of Brazil's labour force was living in small towns and working on a casual basis in the farm sector (de Janvry et al., 1986).

In other parts of Latin America which have already implemented some kind of agrarian reform or land distribution, the old *hacendado* is now replaced by new corporate entrepreneurs and managers who run their estates from skyscrapers in such cities as São Paulo, Santiago, Bogotá, Caracas, Mexico City and San Salvador and commute to their estates by helicopters and Lear jets.

The peasant/former *colonato*/now part wage worker lives a precarious existence, whether in a Mexican *ejido* farm or adjacent to a coffee plantation in Brazil or Costa Rica. The agricultural labour force and the rural population more generally is already a minority in Latin America; in Chile (17%), Peru (32%), Colombia (33%), Venezuela (15%) and Mexico (31%), the rural proportion of the population is low. The agricultural labour force, as may be seen from Table 4, is nevertheless a larger proportion of the labour force than the urban population is of the total population, indicating that agriculture remains an important employer for a fast-growing population of working age. The relatively slow growth of industrial employment and the inappropriate technology choices of the modern sector leave agriculture as a source of labour absorption along with the informal/service sector of the towns and rural areas. For most South American countries, except Bolivia and Paraguay, agriculture accounts for less than 40% of the labour force, while in Central America, except in Costa Rica, agriculture is for most countries still the principal source of employment and thus makes the region more receptive to popular mobilizations. It is, therefore, not surprising that peasant-based insurgencies challenged state and local power in a number of Central American countries during the 1980s.

Similarly in the Middle East, agriculture is now a minority sector in labour force terms in Algeria (31%), Tunisia (30%) and Syria (32%) where the farm sector is fast declining in economic importance. Only in Egypt is 46% of the labour force still absorbed in agriculture and 54% of the population still living in villages, though agriculture accounts for only 20% of GDP. Egypt's rural economy therefore still remains a source of backwardness and poverty, despite the Nasser regime's agrarian reforms.

In Asia and Africa, agriculture remains the main source of livelihood for all except a few fast growing industrial economies such as South Korea and Taiwan. However, in most of Africa, peasant mobilizations would be pointless in the absence of an indigenous class of landlords or even a clearly articulated capitalist class. In the colonial period, when white settler control of the land was a source of grievance, and indeed sparked off the Mau Mau rebellion in Kenya, such mobilization took on nationalist overtones and became part of the anti-colonial struggle. In the post-colonial phase, settler lands have been appropriated in one fell swoop in Angola and Mozambique, or have been progressively appropriated in Kenya and Zimbabwe, so that they hardly figured as targets for peasant mobilizations. Only in Kenya is there a tendency for a visible target to emerge in the shape of the new Kenyan capitalist farmer taking over the white settler estates while a large landless proletariat is growing up as a by-product of the creation of a differentiated peasantry. Here again the peasants and small rural capitalists created by the distribution of settler lands, as in Zimbabwe and Kenya, are creating new centres of power in the rural areas whose interests stand in contradiction to those who have not benefited from the redistribution of settler lands.

In South Asia, as indeed in South-East Asia, the landlord/capitalist/rich farmer is the new centre of power in the countryside. Whilst the oppression and exploitation inflicted by this class are no less severe than that associated with the old feudal order, they have been more diffused and hence more difficult to identify as targets for the mobilization of the poorest peasants. Whilst peasant movements of varying degrees of effectiveness have developed in India over the last three decades, in Pakistan, Bangladesh and even in Sri Lanka peasant insurgency as such has been non-existent since the 1940s. Even the rural JVP rebellion in Sri Lanka in 1971 was, in fact, an insurrection by rural petty-bourgeois youth (Gunasinghe, 1982). Nor have there been any peasant mobilizations in Indonesia since the decimation of its Communist Party in 1965. In both Indonesia and Thailand, as indeed in Malaysia, not discussed here, a new class of rich farmer/capitalist has emerged as the dominant force in the village and retains a much more tenable hold on rural power.

It is only in the Philippines that a continuing peasant mobilization has surfaced to challenge not just the autocracy of the erstwhile Marcos regime but the massive inequalities in access to land and resources left untouched by the 1972 agrarian reform. The 37% of landless households and 23% of the land-poor households (with less than one hectare) are the constituency for the Communist-led insurgency in the Philippines. However the targets in the Filipino countryside remain more diffused since, at least in the paddy and corn lands covered by the Marcos reforms, no large landowners remain, except in the corporate rice farms. The incumbent landlords leasing out their small plots of land (in average sizes of 1.2 hectares to some 30.8% of permanent leasehold tentants) in 1972 accounted for 22% of all farms (Sobhan, 1983). This class of small landowners could hardly be the target of a peasant mobilization. If such a target could be identifiable, it is likely to be the corporate sugar *haciendas* and the foreign-owned commercial crop plantations. Even in the unreformed coconut lands, where large holdings still remain, the average holding is around five hectares.

The target of a mobilization today is therefore a corporate capitalist farmer who shares state power with the urban-based business classes and professionals. The struggle for a new generation of agrarian reforms in the Philippines is thus likely to be more appropriately resolved at the level of the state rather than through any reconfiguration of power in rural areas. The Aquino administration recognised the threat to the survival of the state from the insurgency and presented a package of agrarian reforms, which aimed to complete the Marcos reforms and further redistribute some land, to the parliament. The reforms appear to have been diluted by the legislature. But it is too early to say if the new regime – let alone its successor elected in 1992 – has the political support within the legislature to carry through any more radical reforms. Indeed, even those reforms which have been enacted appear to be facing problems in their implementation. The turnover of ministers in charge of the Aquino agrarian reforms suggested that all was not well and that the Filipino landowning classes still have the political strength to frustrate any radical agrarian reforms.

The future for agrarian reform

The evidence from around the developing world suggests that, as it stands, there are very few countries where radical reform is on the political agenda. In Latin America, where the scope and economic logic for a redistributive reform within the prevailing relations of production is strongest, in very few countries do we see signs of a political mobilization to carry through such reforms, and nowhere are radical reforms of the Cuban or Chinese variety disturbing the sleep of the entrenched rural elite.

In Latin America, Africa and the Middle East no significant political pressures are being exercised from political beneficiaries of such reforms, even though in most of Latin America a constituency for such a mobilization is emerging, if no longer as powerful as it used to be.

Only in Asia – in Bangladesh, Pakistan and India, together with the Philippines and possibly Indonesia – does an identified constituency of the dispossessed exist with the potential to challenge the power of the landed elites. The class of the landless and land-poor, the sharecropper-cum-agricultural worker have demonstrated some capacity for mobilization, positively in parts of India and now with increasing effectiveness in the Philippines. However outside the Philippines even the most committed peasant activist would be hard put to argue that a decisive transformation in the balance of power in favour of poor peasants is on the cards in the near future.

The limited prospects for peasant mobilization in support of radical agrarian reforms is in part due to the failure of political leaders to exploit the persistence of poverty and despair evident in most peasant societies of the Third World today. This failure has varying explanations originating in the specific historical experiences of particular countries. Any analysis of such mobilizations, what happened to them and their current weaknesses, demands serious study. In particular such study should concentrate on what scope really exists for effecting changes in the balance of internal power, which as we have seen is an essential condition for realizing a transformation in the circumstances of the rural poor.

It has, indeed, been the burden of our argument in this book that these failures in peasant mobilization are themselves related to the changed balance of power in rural society in the post-reform countryside. The new elites, whether in Latin America, South or South-East Asia, are more numerous, more deeply entrenched in the rural community and in the vanguard of technological change. They have a pervasive economic control over the peasantry through their command of factor markets other than land. Redistribution of land has failed to dislodge these elites because it had not disturbed this class's monopolies in other markets. Today a minifundist land reform beneficiary still has to go to the rich farmer-cum-moneylender for credit, irrigation water, inputs supplied by a privatised distribution system and, above all, work and land for rent so as to utilize his surplus labour. The impact of new agricultural production technologies has thus opened up new dimensions to the nature of power and its distribution in rural society.

This relationship between the new rural elite and poor peasants may be increasingly mediated by the market, but in rural societies where feudalism has deep roots, aspects of this relationship will remain permeated by non-market features whereby access to land and work will be traded for political support and household services. Faced with a dominant class whose resources are more diversified and powers more sophisticated than those available to the landlord of the *ancien régime*, the peasant mobiliser is hard put to rally the poor to challenge the power of the entrenched elites. True, any number of local struggles led by a variety of activists have achieved some modicum of success in their localities, but this has rarely threatened the overall power of the state.

The arena of struggle has thus moved to the state where new dominant rural elites are in most cases part of a ruling class in coalition with the predominantly urban business sector and/or foreign capital. It is this class which now claims to speak for the rural poor, whether in parliament or other forums. It is through this class that the state reaches the poor peasant politically and administratively. This situation does not rule out mobilization which seeks to establish the effective presence of the rural poor either in the legislature or as a significant object of concern in the eyes of the decision-makers, but the recorded outcome of such mobilizations, whatever the historical reasons may be, has not been very remarkable.

Reformism rather than agrarian reform?

Where does this leave the agenda for agrarian reform as we approach the end of the century? As in Latin America, where the system of functional dualism keeps the rural poor captive in the market place as a supply of cheap labour to the rural capitalist sector, or in Asia, where share-cropping cum wage labour has become essential to enable capitalist farmers to reap the gains of technological diffusion, the new rural elites have an interest in preserving differentiation in the countryside. Further distribution of land, which was tolerated in the days when technological and investment options for the *hacendado* were limited, are no longer on the cards except through access to limited amounts of new or frontier land, where such are available. However, even such supplies of new land which threaten to drain away the cheap labour available would hardly be in the interest of the new capitalist elites. Thus the hopes of an earlier generation that sought painlessly to eliminate an externally patronised and functionally useless class from its domination of the large under-cultivated latifundias can no longer sustain present day aspirant reformists.

In the absence of peasant mobilizations of the Chinese variety, hopes for land reform will have to ride on the prospects of a political coalition capturing state power which is neither drawn from nor depends for support on the rural elites. The post-1968 military regime in Peru was of such a character and could thus carry through far-reaching reforms, but it could not fully eliminate rural differentiation and landlessness or radically reduce poverty. If we look to other developing countries, such coalitions remain difficult to identify. We may thus be left with the current strategy of accepting differentiation in the countryside as given. Development programmes may continue, with perhaps more effectiveness to reach out to the poor than hitherto demonstrated. Where surplus lands exist, as in parts of Latin America, Indonesia and the Philippines, these may be incorporated in land distribution as distinct from agrarian reform programmes, though limits to this will obviously be set because of its threat to the dualism that prevails. Where tenancy arrangements exist attempts marginally to improve crop shares and provide some security of tenure may be made, but here too the implications of such a move in making labour more expensive will generate resistance from elites who will strive to control both access to new lands and the diffusion of new technology.

Thus rural poverty, under-employment and landlessness are likely to remain with us and be subject to erosion only in some of the fastest-growing of the newly industrializing countries. For the rest, we will have to address our attention to the dynamics of peasant mobilization and social transformation if we are to seek answers to the hopes of eradicating rural poverty.

This study remains at its conclusion firmly committed to its central premise, that if the goal is to eliminate rural poverty and accelerate all-round economic developments, there is no alternative to a radical agrarian reform which redistributes land widely enough to incorporate the bulk of the landless and land-poor in its ambit and which thereby totally eliminates the current as well as any potential new dominant class in the countryside. This holds even where land distribution may create minifundist holdings. We have seen that these smallholdings can be sustained by socializing the labour surplus to the needs of the holding and using it in a planned way for a variety of non-farm investments and providing through co-operatives of land reform beneficiary access to factor markets once monopolised by the elites. The inevitable expansion of rural markets as a result of such a reform will provide the dynamic for rural industrialization and the development of modern industry. As we have seen in the cases of South Korea, Taiwan etc, such a reform may be carried out without prejudice to the continuation of the dominant mode of production outside agriculture, but it will need an unusual constellation of forces to recreate the East Asian historical situation in which a socially undifferentiated countryside could co-exist with a capitalist and inegalitarian urban industrial sector.

Bibliography

Abdel-Malek, A. *Egypt: Military Society, The Army Regime, the Left and Social Change Under Nasser* (New York, Vintage Books, 1968).

Ahmed, S. 'Landlessness in Rural Asia', *Land Reform, Land Settlement and Cooperatives* (Rome, FAO). 1987 (mimeo).

Bakx, K. 'Planning Agrarian Reform: Amazonian Settlement Projects, 1970–86', *Development and Change* (Hague, ISS) Oct. 1987.

Bearman, J. *Qadaffi's Libya* (London, Zed Books, 1986).

Berry, R. A. and W. R. Cline, *Agrarian Structure and Productivity in Developing Countries* (Baltimore, Johns Hopkins University Press, 1979).

Bettelheim, C., *Cultural Revolution and Industrial Organisation in China* (Monthly Review Press, New York, 1968).

Bezzabeh, M. 'A Review of Recent Trends in Agrarian Reform and Rural Development in Tropical Africa', *Land Report* (Rome, FAO, 1981) No. 1/2.

Black, G. *Triumph of the People: The Sandinista Revolution in Nicaragua* (London, Zed Books, 1981).

Bokhari, A. S. *Evaluation of Agrarian Reform Measures in Pakistan* (Dhaka, CIRDAP, 1986; mimeograph).

Brundenius, C. *Revolutionary Cuba: The Challenge of Economic Growth with Equity* (Boulder, Westview Press, 1984).

Caracatus, *Revolution in Iraq* (London, Victor Gollancz, 1959).

Cassen, R., et al. *Does Aid Work?* (Oxford: OUP, 1986).

Castillo, L. & D. Lehman, 'Agrarian Reform and Structural Change in Chile, 1975–79' in A. K. Ghose (ed.) *Agrarian Reform in Contemporary Developing Countries* (Beckenham, Croom Helm, 1983).

Chaliand, G. *The Peasants of North Vietnam* (Harmondsworth, Penguin Books, 1969).

Chaney, E. *Agrarian Reform and Politics* (Wisconsin, Land Tenure Center, 1970, mimeograph LTC No. 74).

Chakravarty, S. 'Power Structure and Agricultural Productivity' in M. Desai et al. *Agrarian Power and Agricultural Productivity in South Asia* (Berkeley, University of California Press, 1984).

Chao, K. *Economic Effects of Land Reforms in Taiwan, Japan and Mainland China: A Comparative Study*, (Wisconsin University PB-223 788, 1972).

Chenery, H. and M. Ahluwalia, *Redistribution with Growth* (Oxford, OUP, 1974)

CIRDAP *Evaluation of Agrarian Reform Measures in Bangladesh* (Dhaka, CIRDAP, 1987, CIRDAP Study Series 89, mimeograph).

Class Struggles in the USSR, Vol. 1, 1917–23 (1976) and Vol. 2, 1923–30 (1978) (Harvester Press, Sussex).

Cliffe, L. *Policy Options for Agrarian Reform in Zimbabwe* (Rome, FAO, 1986, mimeograph).

Dobb, M. H. *Soviet Economic Development Since 1917* (London, Routledge and Kegan Paul, 1948).

Dorner, P. *Land Reform and Economic Development* (Harmondsworth, Penguin Books, 1982).

Dumont, R. and M. Mazoyer, *Socialism and Development* (London, André Deutsch, 1973).

El-Zoobi, A. M. *Alleviation of Rural Poverty Through Agrarian Reform and Rural Development in the Syrian Arab Republic* (Rome, FAO, 1984, In-depth Study Series No. 17).

FAO *Studies on Agrarian Reform and Rural Poverty* (Rome, FAO, 1984).

FAO *The Effects of Land Tenure and Fragmentation of Farm Holdings on Agricultural Development* (Rome, FAO, 1986, mimeograph).

FAO *Second Progress Report on WCARRD Programme of Action Including the Role of Women in Rural Development* (Rome, FAO, 1987).

Gabbay, R. "The Iraqi Communists" Agrarian Programme: from Dialectism to Temporal Conformism' in S. Jones et al., *Rural Poverty and Agrarian Reform* (New Delhi, Allied Publishers, 1982).

Ghose, A. K. (ed.) *Agrarian Reform in Contemporary Developing Countries* (London, Croom Helm, 1983).

Ghose, A. K. 'Agrarian Reforms in West Bengal: Objectives, Achievements and Limitations' in A. K. Ghose, *Agarian Reform in Developing Countries* (London, Croom Helm, 1983).

Ghose, A. K. *The New Development Strategy and Rural Reforms in Post-Mao China* (Geneva, ILO, 1983, World Employment Programme Research Working Paper).

Goulden, J. C. *Korea: The Untold Story of the War* (New York, McGraw-Hill, 1982).

Griffin, K. *The Political Economy of Agrarian Change* (London, Macmillan, 1974).

Gunasinghe, N. 'Land Reform, Class Structure and the State in Sri Lanka 1970–77' in S. Jones et al., *Rural Poverty and Agrarian Reform* (New Delhi, Allied Publishers, 1982).

Halliday, F. *Arabia Without Sultans* (Harmondsworth, Penguin Books, 1974).

Hanxian, L. *Economic Changes in Rural China* (Beijing, New World Press, 1985).

Haque, T. and A. S. Sirohi, *Agrarian Reforms and Institutional Changes in India* (New Delhi, Concept Publishing Co., 1986).

Herring, R. J. *Land to the Tiller: The Political Economy of Agrarian Reform in South Asia* (New Haven, Yale University Press, 1985).

Hinton, W. *Fanshen: A Documentary of Revolution in a Chinese Village* (New York, Monthly Review Press, 1968).

Hinton, W. *Shenfan: The Continuing Revolution in a Chinese Village* (New York, Vintage Books, 1984).

Hirashima, S. and M. Muqtada, *Hired Labour and Rural Labour Markets in Asia* (New Delhi, ILO-ARTEP, 1986).

Hossain, M. *Green Revolution in Bangladesh: Its Nature and Impact on Income Distribution* (Dhaka, BIDS Working Paper No. 4, 1987).

Hunt, D. *The Impending Crisis in Kenya: The Case for Land Reform* (Aldershot, Gower Publishing Co., 1984).

Huizer, G. *Peasant Mobilisation and Land Reform in Indonesia* (The Hague, ISS, 1972, ISS Occasional Papers, mimeograph).

Inayatullah, (ed.) *Land Reform: Some Asian Experiences* (Kuala Lumpur, APDC, 1980).

ILO *World Labour Report* 3 (Geneva, ILO, 1987).

ILO *Strategies for Promoting Rural Employment* (Geneva, ILO, 1987).

Jannuzi, F. T. and J. T. Peach, *The Agrarian Structure of Bangladesh* (New Delhi, Sangam Books, 1982).

de Janvry, A. *The Agrarian Question and Reformism in Latin America* (Baltimore, Johns Hopkins University Press, 1981).

de Janvry, A., E. Sadoulet & L. Wilcox, *Rural Labour in Latin America* (Geneva, ILO, 1986, mimeograph. World Employment Programme Research Working Paper).

Joshi, P. C. *Land Reforms in India* (Bombay, Allied Publishers, 1975).

Kay, C. 'The Agrarian Reform in Peru: An Assessment' in A. K. Ghose, *Agrarian Reform in Developing Countries* (London, Croom Helm, 1983).

Khan, M. H. *Underdevelopment and Agrarian Structure in Pakistan* (Boulder, Westview Press, 1981).

Khan, M. H. *Lectures on Agrarian Transformation in Pakistan* (Islamabad, PIDE, 1985).

Kimche, J. *Seven Fallen Pillars* (London, Secker and Warburg, 1950).

King, R. *Land Reform: A World Survey* (London, Bell & Son, 1977).

King, D. J. *Land Reform and Participation of the Rural Poor in the Development Process in African Countries* (Wisconsin, LTC No. 10, 1974).

Koo, A. Y. C. *Land Market Distortion and Tenure Reform* (Ames, Iowa State University Press, 1982).

Ledesma, A. J. *Land Reform Programs in East and South East Asia: A Comparative Approach* Madison, LTC, 1976 (Mimeograph).

Lehman, D. (ed.) *Agrarian Reform and Agrarian Reformism* (London, Faber and Faber, 1974).

Lehman, D. 'The Death of Land Reform: A Polemic', *World Development* (Oxford, March 1968).

Lipton, M. 'Towards a Theory of Land Reform', in D. Lehman (ed.), *Agrarian Reform and Agrarian Reformism* (London, Faber and Faber, 1974).

Lewin, M. *Russian Peasants and Soviet Power* (London, George Allen and Unwin, 1968).

Lippit, V. *Land Reform and Economic Development in China* (White Plains, IASP, 1974).

MacEwan, A. 'Revolution, Agrarian Reform and Economic Transformation in Cuba' in S. Jones et al. (eds), *Rural Poverty and Agrarian Reform* (Bombay, Allied Publishers, 1982).

Mangahas, M., V. Miralao & R. P. de los Reyes, *Tenants, Lessees, Owners, Welfare Implications of Tenure Change* (Manila, IPC, 1976).

Manituzzaman, T. *Military Withdrawal from Politics: A Comparative Study* (Dhaka, University Press Ltd, 1987).

Masang, B. *Evaluation of Agrarian Reform Measures in Thailand* (Dhaka, CIRDAP, 1986, mimeograph).

McCormack, G. & J. Gittings (eds) *Crisis in Korea*, (Nottingham, Spokesman Books, 1977).

Meliczek, H. *Agrarian Reform in the Philippines* (Manila, FAO/UNDP, 1980).

Ministry of Agriculture, Socialist Republic of Vietnam, *Evaluation of Agrarian Reform Measures in Vietnam* (Dhaka, CIRDAP, 1986, mimeograph).

Mitra, A. *Terms of Trade and Class Relations* (London, Frank Cass, 1979).

Murmis, M. 'Agrarian Reform Under Landowner Initiative: The Case of the Ecuadorian Highlands', in S. Jones et al. (eds), *Rural Poverty and Agrarian Reform* (Bombay, Allied Publishers, 1982).

Noggo, Y. 'Agrarian Reform and Class Struggle in Ethiopia', *Journal of Social Studies* (Dhaka, July 1984).

Nolan, P. 'Collectivisation in China: Some Comparisons with USSR' in S. Jones et al. (eds), *Rural Poverty and Agrarian Reform* (Bombay, Allied Publishers, 1982).

Open University *Peru 1968–75: Revolution from Above?* Third World Studies, Case Study 10 (Milton Keynes, The Open University Press, 1983).

Panganiban, L. C. and R. G. Maranan, *Evaluation of Agrarian Reform Measures in the Philippines* (Dhaka, CIRDAP, 1986).

Patnaik, U. 'Class Differentiation within the Peasantry', *Economic and Political Weekly* Vol. XI, No. 39, Bombay 1976.

Peek, P. (ed.) *Rural Poverty in Central America: Causes and Poverty Alternatives* (Geneva, ILO, 1986 mimeograph).

Petras, J. F. and R. Laporte, *Cultivating Revolution* (New York, Vintage Books, 1972).

Planck, U. 'Progress and Results of Land Reform in the Middle East', *Land Reform* (Rome, FAO, 1985).

Qayyum, A. 'Policies and Implementation of Land Reforms' in Inayatullah (ed.) *Land Reform: Some Asian Experiences* (Kuala Lumpur, APDC, 1980).

Rahman, H. Z. *Landed Property and the Dynamic of Instability in Bengal: State-formation under Colonialism and its Contemporary Significance* (PhD Thesis, Department of Sociology, University of Manchester, 1986).

Rahman, A., T. Haque & S. Mahmud, *A Critical Review of Poverty in Bangladesh in the 1980s* (Dhaka, BIDS, 1987, mimeograph).

Rahmato, D. *Agrarian Reform in Ethiopia* (Trenton, Red Sea Press, 1985).

Raju, K. N. *Evaluation of Agrarian Reform Measures in India* (Dhaka, CIRDAP, 1986).

Rao, D. 'Economic Growth and Equity in the Republic of Korea', *World Development* (Oxford, March 1978).

Rhee, Sang-Woo, 'Land Reform in South Korea: A Macro Level Policy Review' in Inayatullah (ed.), *Land Reform: Some Asian Experiences* (Kuala Lumpur, APDC, 1980).

Rudolph, L. & S. Rudolph, 'Determinants and Varieties of Agrarian Mobilisation' in M. Desai et al. (ed.), *Agrarian Power and Agricultural Productivity in South Asia* (Berkeley, University of California Press, 1984).

Sanderatne, N. & M. A. Zaman, *The Impact of Agrarian Structure on the Political Leadership of Undivided Pakistan* (Madison, LTC No. 94, 1973).

Schlesinger S. & S. Kinzer, *Bitter Fruit: The Untold Story of the American Coup in Guatemala* (New York, Anchor Books, 1983).

Sen, Amartya, *Poverty and Famines: An Essay on Entitlement and Deprivation* (Oxford, Clarendon Press, 1981).

Sender, J. & S. Smith, *The Development of Capitalism in Africa* (London, Methuen, 1986).

Siddiqui, K. 'The Political Economy of Land Reforms in Bangladesh' in Inayatullah (ed.), *Land Reform: Some Asian Experiences* (Kuala Lumpur, APDC, 1980).

Sigurdson, J. 'Rural Industrialisation: A Comparison of Development Planning in China and India', *World Development* (Oxford, May 1968).

Sinha, R. *Landlessness: A Growing Problem* (Rome, FAO, 1984).

Sobhan, R. *Basic Democracies, Works Programme and Rural Development in East Pakistan* (Dhaka, Oxford University Press, 1968).

Sobhan, R. *The Crisis of External Dependence: The Political Economy of Foreign Aid to Bangladesh* (London, Zed Press, 1982).

Sobhan, R. *Rural Poverty and Agrarian Reform in the Philippines* (In-depth Study Series No. 2, FAO, Rome, 1983).

Sobhan, R. 'Industrialisation and Structural Change in Rural China', *Asian Affairs* (Dhaka, 1986).

Sobhan, R. *Entitlements and Rural Poverty: Trends in Access to Land and Employment* (Rome, ESH Division, FAO, 1986 mimeograph).

Sobhan, R. *Public Allocative Strategies, Rural Development and Poverty Alleviation: A global perspective* (Dhaka, University Press, 1991).

Sobhan R. & T. Islam *Aid Dependence of Consumption: A Sector Level Analysis*, (Dhaka, BIDS, 1987, mimeograph).

Springborg, R. 'Iraqi Infitah: Agrarian Transformation and Growth of the Private Sector', *The Middle East Journal* (Washington DC, Winter 1986).

Sutton, K. 'Agrarian Reform in Algeria' in S. Jones et al, (ed.) *Rural Poverty and Agrarian Reform* (Bombay, Allied Publishers, 1982).

Trap, F. 'Agrarian Transformation in Mozambique'. *Land Reforms, Land Settlement and Cooperatives* (Rome FAO, 1984).

Tuma, E. 'Agrarian Reforms in Historical Perspective Revisited', *Comparative Studies in History and Society* (Cambridge, Jan. 1979).

Turton, A. 'Poverty, Reform and Class Struggle in Thailand' in S. Jones et al. (ed.) *Rural Poverty and Agrarian Reform* (Bombay, Allied Publishers, 1982).

United Nations *Progress in Land Reform*, Fifth Report, 1970; Sixth Report, 1976, (New York, United Nations).

Wahab, A. & G. C. Sen, *Evaluation of Agrarian Reform Measures in Bangladesh* (Dhaka, CIRDAP, 1986).

Walinsky, L. J. (ed.) *Agrarian Reform as Unfinished Business: The Selected Papers of Wolf Ladejinsky* (New York, Oxford University Press, 1977).

Wanigaratne, R. D. *Evaluation of Agrarian Reform (Measures in Sri Lanka)* (Dhaka, CIRDAP, 1986).

Warriner, D. *Revolution in Eastern Europe* (London, Turnstile Press, 1950).

Warriner, D. *Land Reform in Principle and Practise* (Oxford, Clarendon Press, 1969).

Warriner, D. *Results of Land Reform in Asian and Latin American Countries* (Conference on Strategies for Agricultural Development in the 1970s, Stanford University, Dec. 1971).

Whittemore, C. *Land for People: Land Tenure and the Very Poor* (Oxford, Oxfam, 1981).

Wolf, E. R. Jr. *Peasant Wars of the Twentieth Century* (London, Faber and Faber, 1969).

Wong, J. *Land Reform in the People's Republic of China* (New York, Praeger, 1973).

World Bank *Land Reform in Latin America: Bolivia, Chile, Mexico, Peru, Venezuela*, World Bank Staff Working Paper No. 275 (Washington DC, World Bank, 1978).

World Bank *World Development Report 1986 and 1987* (Washington DC, World Bank).

Wurfel, D. 'The Development of Post-War Philippine Land Reform: A Political and Sociological Explanation', *View From the Paddy II* (Manila, IPC, 1982).

Index

absorption of labour, 31, 114
Afghanistan, 7
agrarian reform: case for, 114-23;
  conceptualization of, 16-18;
  devaluation of, 2-3; economic impact
  of, 76-102; efficiency of, 123-5; future
  for, 136-7; in egalitarian economies,
  83-102; in non-egalitarian economies,
  93-102; in South Asia, 56-66; in
  today's conditions, 103-25; political
  feasibility of, 132-7; scope of, 126-38;
  varieties of, 7-20; within capitalist
  mode of production, 52, 72; without
  social transition, 19-20, 49-75
agrarian transition, processes of, 13-16
agricultural policy, 80-3
agricultural production, 95-7;
  improvement of, 97-9
Algeria, 35, 41, 46-8, 74, 93, 94, 97, 101,
  105, 109, 117, 118, 134
Allende regime (Chile), 50, 101
Alliance for Progress, 52
Amazonia, 116
Anand Dairy Co-operative, 123
Angola, 35, 46-8, 94-5, 117, 118, 134
Aquino administration (Philippines), 135
Arbenz regime (Guatemala), 53, 54,
Argentina, 87, 108, 119
autogestion, 47, 97

Baath Socialist Party (Syria), 45, 46
Bandaranaike administration (Sri
  Lanka), 62
Bangladesh, 49, 57-60, 66, 71, 94, 100,
  101, 103, 104, 105, 108, 116, 118, 125,
  130, 131, 135, 136
Bettelheim, Charles, 13
Bhutto regime (Pakistan), 60-1
Bolivia, 3, 35, 37-8, 50, 66, 93, 94, 95, 100,
  101, 102, 103, 104, 115, 118, 127, 134
Brazil, 66, 101, 104, 108, 112, 116, 117,

125, 126, 127, 132, 133, 134
Bukharin, Nikolai, 119
Bulgaria, 81

Cambodia, 7
capitalism, 15; definition of, 14
capitalist agriculture, 63-6
Cardenas, President, 98
cash crops, 62, 79, 115, 116
Castro, Fidel, 27
Central Intelligence Agency (CIA), 54
Chile, 3, 49-51, 63, 97, 100, 101, 102, 103,
  104, 105, 108, 117, 122, 127, 134
China, 1, 2, 3, 4, 16, 17, 22, 24, 26, 27, 33,
  83, 84, 86, 88, 89, 90, 111, 122, 123,
  124, 126, 130, 131, 136, 137
collective farms, 26, 33, 40, 50, 73, 80, 82,
  84, 90, 93, 102, 110, 117, 122, 124;
  dismantling of, 3
Colombia, 49, 51, 55, 104, 108, 134
colonatos, 14, 35, 50, 78, 95, 96, 134
Costa Rica, 49, 52, 55, 104, 108, 116, 134
cropping patterns, changes in, 79, 80, 115,
  116, 117, 128
Cuba, 13, 16, 22, 24, 27-9, 50, 52, 56, 83,
  84, 87, 91, 99, 104, 117, 122, 123, 136
Cultural Revolution (China), 86

decollectivization, 2
decolonization: and class formation, 75;
  as road to agrarian reform, 46-8
demographic pressure, 31, 37, 104-5, 109,
  129
differentiation, rural, 22, 31, 32, 44, 46,
  100-2
Dulles, John Foster, 54

Ecuador, 49, 51, 105, 108
Egypt, 3, 35, 41, 42-3, 85, 93, 94, 95, 100,
  102, 103, 104, 105, 109, 113, 118, 125,
  129-30, 134

ejido farms, 38, 55, 93, 98, 99, 134
El Salvador, 49, 52, 53, 104, 105
Ethiopia, 3, 22, 32-4, 92-3, 105, 122, 126, 131
expropriation of land, 30, 31, 32, 33, 36, 50, 51, 53, 54, 62, 63, 67, 73, 94

fertilizer, use of, 92, 105
feudalism, 3, 15, 18, 25, 26, 27, 30, 31, 32, 38, 41, 43, 46, 50, 57, 58, 59, 60-2, 65, 95, 137; definition of, 14
Food for Work programmes, 113
food production, restructuring of, 119
foreign aid, 1, 110
foreign exchange, 81, 98, 125

Ghana, 116
green revolution, 58, 59, 60, 64, 65, 71, 98, 102, 108, 115
Guatemala, 49, 52, 53-4, 56, 78, 104, 105, 108

hacendados, 13, 14, 15, 35, 36, 38, 40, 50, 51, 55, 62, 66, 69, 70, 96, 98, 102, 108, 119, 125, 133
haciendas, 14, 37, 40, 45, 54, 56, 69, 78, 93, 94, 128, 135; break-up of, 128; conversion of, 117
high-yield varieties, 60, 68, 108
Ho Chi Minh, 25
Honduras, 49, 52, 55-6, 104, 105
Household Responsibility System, 111, 124
hunos, 59

India, 49, 57, 63-6, 71, 79, 94, 95, 100, 101, 103, 104, 108, 112, 113, 116, 118, 122, 130, 131, 136
Indonesia, 49, 66, 100, 104, 112, 125, 131, 135, 136, 138
industrialization, 1, 3, 109, 111, 112
inquilinos, 50
Integrated Rural Development Programmes (IRDP), 3, 113
International Monetary Fund (IMF), 98
investment, 17, 18, 43, 81, 85, 92, 104, 111, 116, 124, 128
Iraq, 35, 41, 42, 43-4, 94, 96, 97, 102, 105, 129
irrigation, 43, 44, 85, 96, 99, 104, 105, 110, 136

Japan, 3, 4, 7, 16, 24, 25, 26, 29-32, 84, 85, 88, 89, 117, 131

Kennedy administration (US), 52

Kenya, 49, 72-3, 94, 95, 100, 103, 105, 112, 115, 116, 118, 128, 129, 134
Kerala state, 131, 132; agrarian reform in, 65
Khan, Mahmud Hasan, 61
Kim Il Sung, 26
Korea, North, 3, 16, 22, 24, 26-7, 33, 83, 85, 87, 89, 90, 111, 112, 122, 126, 131
Korea, South, 3, 4, 7, 16, 22, 29-32, 84, 85, 86, 88, 89, 90, 102, 104, 105, 108, 110, 112, 117, 122, 131, 134, 138
kulaks, control of, 82

labour, absorption of, 109-13
land: access to, 16, 18, 20, 123; distribution of, 4, 12, 21, 22, 27, 29, 30, 31, 33, 36, 43, 47, 49, 56, 60, 68, 78, 81, 109, 118, 123, 126-7, 129, 130, 136, 138
land to the tiller, 32, 67, 94, 132
landlessness, 12, 13, 16, 18, 22, 27, 29, 36, 40, 43, 46, 48, 68, 99, 100, 102, 103-4, 113, 114, 127, 129, 135
landlords, absentee, 39, 45, 47, 58, 62, 68, 69, 71, 96, 102
landowners, 1, 13, 14, 15, 18, 24, 25, 29, 30, 31, 36, 42, 45, 57, 58, 67, 70; resistance of, 53, 55
Laos, 7
Libya, 41, 42, 87

Malaysia, 116, 117, 118
Marcos regime (Philippines), 69, 101, 132, 135
marketable surplus, question of, 117-22
Mau Mau rebellion (Kenya), 72, 134
mechanization, 91, 104, 116
Mexico, 3, 35, 38, 50, 55, 66, 87, 93, 94, 95, 97, 98, 99, 101, 102, 103, 104, 105, 108, 110, 112, 115, 118, 125, 127, 134
micro-surveys, 77, 78
minifundism, 2, 12, 15, 17, 32, 40, 41, 45, 47, 63, 64, 65, 80, 89, 90, 99, 110, 114, 122, 136
Morocco, 129
Mozambique, 35, 46-8, 72, 94, 95, 96, 105, 117, 118, 134
Mugabe administration (Zimbabwe), 74, 129
Muslim League (East Pakistan), 57
Myanmar, 7, 35

Nasser, Gamal Abdul, 42, 134
nationalization of land, 46, 47, 74
New Economic Policy (NEP) (USSR), 82
Nicaragua, 3, 35, 38-40, 55, 56, 96, 104, 105, 118, 125, 133

Nigeria, 125

Pakistan, 7, 49, 57, 58, 59, 60-2, 64, 66, 71,
    79, 94, 95, 100, 101, 103, 105, 108, 113,
    116, 117, 118, 119, 130, 131, 135, 136
Panama, 52, 55-6, 105, 108
Paraguay, 108, 133, 134
peasant capitalism, 66-71
peasants: market responsiveness of, 116;
    mobilization of, 1, 18, 19, 25-6, 27, 32,
    33, 35-41, 52, 54, 67, 83, 124, 129, 133,
    135, 136, 137; tenacity of, 66
People's Party (Pakistan), 61
Peru, 3, 35, 38, 40-1, 50, 63, 66, 94, 95, 97,
    100, 102, 103, 104, 105, 117, 127, 134,
    137
Philippines, 49, 59, 66, 69-71, 77, 94, 95,
    100, 101, 103, 104, 108, 116, 117, 118,
    131, 132, 135, 136, 138
poverty, 17, 114; rural, 1, 2, 4, 20, 104,
    109, 115 (eradication of, 113-14)
Preobrazhensky, Evgeni, 2, 81, 82, 119
pricing policy, 84, 85, 92, 124
productivity, relative, 115-17

reformism, 137-8
resources, public, access to, 88-9

Sandinista administration (Nicaragua),
    39, 133
Selassie, Haile, 32, 133
service co-operatives, 114
sharecropping, 16, 29, 57, 58-60, 62, 70,
    71, 95, 102, 136, 137
small farms, 39, 44, 45, 79, 109, 118, 123,
    131; diseconomies of, 89; efficiency of,
    116
socialist mode of production, 13
Soekarno regime (Indonesia), 67
Somoza family (Nicaragua), 38-9, 96, 133
squatters, 51, 52
Sri Lanka, 49, 57, 62-3, 66, 71, 100, 101,
    103, 104, 105, 108, 118, 130, 131, 135
Stalin, Joseph, 81, 82
state farms, 28, 39, 117
state lands, 44; distribution of, 55;
    reclamation of, 51
structural change in economies, 1, 89
Syria, 35, 41, 42, 44-5, 87, 94, 96, 102, 104,
    105, 129, 134

Taiwan, 3, 4, 7, 16, 22, 29-32, 58, 84, 85,
    88, 89, 104, 105, 110, 112, 117, 134, 138
Tanzania, 122
technology, 3, 18, 48, 115; diffusion of,
    123; new, in agriculture, 108-9

tenure arrangements, 49; reforms of,
    131-2
Thailand, 49, 66, 68, 95, 100, 118, 119,
    131, 135
tribal system of land cultivation, 72
tribal tenure patterns, 12, 47
Tunisia, 49, 74, 94, 100, 104, 134

under-employment, 113; rural, 105
Union of Soviet Socialist Republics
    (USSR), 2, 3, 80, 82, 83, 84, 110, 112,
    117, 119, 122
United Arab Emirates, 87
United Fruit Company, 53, 54
United States of America (USA), 27, 28,
    29-32
Uruguay, 108

Venezuela, 49, 50, 51, 55, 104, 134
Vietnam, 1, 3, 13, 16, 22, 24, 25, 27, 33,
    84, 87, 90, 91, 111, 112, 122, 126, 131;
    North, 26, 83; South, 85

wage labour, 2, 13, 14, 15, 28, 36, 38, 41,
    43, 44, 60, 62, 65, 70, 71, 73, 74, 77, 91,
    102, 104, 132, 136, 137
wages, 113; rural, 108, 109, 114
white settler estates, 72, 73, 74, 94, 128
works programmes, 3
World Bank, 87

Yemen, South, 41

zamindars, 15, 58, 61, 62, 130
Zimbabwe, 49, 94, 105, 118, 125, 128,
    129, 134